CUTTING CORNERS

A Complete College Handbook For Getting A's The Easy Way

By Justin Rich

Copyright © 2012 Justin Rich
All rights reserved.

ISBN: 0984723900
ISBN-13: 9780984723904

For more tips, bonus material, and the latest updates,
visit http://www.cuttingcornersbook.com

To Dad, Mom, Cassie, Phoebe, Cody, and Domenick.

Thank you so much for all of your help.

Contents

Introduction vii

Section 1 – Reshaping Your College Experience 1

1 – What Does Everybody Else Think? 3
2 – Four Life-Changing Concepts to Start With Right Away 13

Section 2 – Assignments 27

3 – Polishing Your Grammar Skills 29
4 – Step Up Your Vocab 39
5 – Ripping Up Papers – Writing 101 41
6 – How to Write a Paper on a Book You Haven't Read 53
7 – Bullshitting Homework Assignments 57
8 – Dealing With Group Assignments 61

Section 3 – Studying 71

9 – Study Habits 73
10 – Memorized Knowledge 85
11 – Learned Knowledge 93
12 – Review Time 103

Section 4 – The Day (and Night Before) the Test 111

13 – Getting Ready Before the Test 113
14 – Taking the Test 129
15 – Extra Questions You May Have Regarding Tests 149

Section 5 – Extra Credit 153

16 – Fun Games to Play During Class 155
17 – How to Sound Like You Know What You're
　　　Talking About During Class.. 161
18 – How to Beg, Plead, and Lose All Integrity
　　　So You Can Get a Better Grade.. 165

Final Words.. 173
Keep the Game Going Online 175

Introduction

Of all the stages that a person goes through in his or her lifetime, you'd be hard-pressed to find one more challenging than the college experience. On the bright side, you've got your "after school" life, which is filled with crazy parties, epic all-you-can-eat dining hall feasts, and organized sports that instill university spirit. But it's not all fun and games. You've also got papers to write, deadlines to meet, and a whole bunch of studying to do. College life can be the biggest hassle in the world at times.

The age-old question of, *""Why can't I just do the fun stuff, and keep the boring stuff to a minimum?"* is something that millions of college students across the nation ask themselves every semester. Most students assume that that's just the way the college system is, and that you can't have one part without the other.

Well, ladies and gentlemen, it's time to turn the college system on its head.

Everything contained in the following pages has been written to show you how to spend as little time as possible on the worthless assignments, tests, and group projects that you might be subjected to in college. By following the advice in this book, you'll be able to spend as much time as you want enjoying the brighter side of college life, while keeping the boring side to a minimum.

I subscribe to the notion that college is supposed to be a time where you explore your freedom and develop a self-identity. Unfortunately, most universities make you jump through hoops just like your high school did.

If you're going to school to study Accounting, why the hell should you have to take a Geology course? You shouldn't. But, too bad for you. You're going to waste your time studying rock formations anyway because it's part of the "curriculum" or the "general education requirements" created by your university.

Fuck that. And fuck them.

This is where this book comes in. Whether you're an extremely motivated student who can find a way to persevere through the mind-numbing subject of Geology without the need for it to be fun, or you're the type who can only study boring stuff when you're high, I've got you covered.

Everything you'll learn in this book has been designed to enhance your college experience. If you're just looking for a more efficient way to study, then you'll get a plethora of useful and immediately applicable advice. If you're looking to slack off and bullshit your way through college by learning the bare minimum, then you've come to the right place too.

I want to make a couple of quick points before we begin. First, I want to make it clear that I'm not against learning. This book wasn't written to piss on the institution of college. There are a lot of great schools and professors out there that exist to teach and to cultivate passion in their students, and I take my hat off to them.

That being said, this book was written to deal with an entirely different set of institutions and people – universities where the students are treated as numbers and statistics, and bureaucratic professors who show up only to collect paychecks and could care less what their students learn.

The second point I'll make is that this is actually a serious book. As humorous as a lot of the topics in this book are, and as much as I'll say the words "fuck" and "shit," all of the advice and all of the techniques contained in these pages are tested and sound methods that you can rely on when it's time to get down to business.

Everything included in this book will sharpen your studying and school-related skills while reducing the time you spend on schoolwork at the same time. There's no doubt about it – this book will improve your grades.

Cutting Corners is divided into five easy-to-read sections, with each section covering one facet of the college experience. Here's what you're going to read:

Section 1 – Reshaping Your College Experience

We'll take a good, hard look at the pressures that everyone faces in school. After that, we'll work on re-framing the way you approach your academic schedule so you can actually have a life. You'll figure out and define what it is that you want out of your college experience. I'll help you customize your approach so you can free up your schedule and make school as stress-free as possible.

Section 2 – Assignments

Do you have trouble writing papers for class? Do you get frustrated when you have to deal with obnoxious tools during group assignments? All of the answers to your issues with college assignments are spelled out for you in an easy way during this section. You'll save countless hours after picking up on the concepts outlined here.

Section 3 – Studying

In this big section, you'll start by discovering new ways to motivate yourself and get into the right habits so that you can study more efficiently. Then, we'll go through a variety of studying techniques that will help you to retain information like you never have before.

You'll learn how to associate the material you need to know for a test with references from your own life, pop culture, and your favorite movies and songs. You'll also learn how to digest and comprehend the major concepts for your test the right way. You'll end this section having all of the skills you need to prep for the big day.

Section 4 – The Day (and Night Before) the Test

Since exams can often account for your entire grade in a class, you need to be serious when the time comes to take a test. In this section, I'll walk you through the entire process - from how much to study right before the test, to how to handle the mind games that professors will play with you on multiple choice questions. By the time you're done, you'll feel comfortable and prepared for any test you'll encounter in the future.

Section 5 – Extra Credit

Here you'll find miscellaneous short chapters that will further enhance your college experience. Among other topics, there's a chapter on fun games to play with your friends if you get stuck going to a boring class, and there's a chapter on how to make it sound like you know what you're talking about during class when you haven't been paying attention.

I know that reading a full book on this stuff sounds like a big time investment. Don't worry about it. Within each section, the book has been broken up into a series of short, easy-to-read chapters. The chapters pretty much stand on their own too. So, if you're only looking to improve certain facets of your college game, feel free to skip around.

Who am I? I'm a fly on the wall who's tired of seeing students struggle with bullshit year after year. My real name isn't Justin Rich. But I've been around the block. You can think of me kind of like a big bro in a fraternity who knows all the ropes and always seems to have a new trick up his sleeve, or your smarty pants friend who is constantly figuring out new ways to beat the system.

Are you ready to embark on this journey? Without further ado, let's get this party started.

Section 1: Reshaping Your College Experience

CHAPTER 1

What Does Everybody Else Think?

Whether or not you realize it yet, all of the people you've been surrounded by your entire life have played a pretty big part in shaping your attitude toward approaching school. The "other players" in your life right now – the university, your professors, your peers, and your parents – have their own agendas. Some of these guys are out to help you, some could care less about you, and some are grasping at straws trying to figure out what to do themselves. The mish-mash of all of these other people's opinions can pull you in different directions when you're trying to figure out how to be a successful student.

"Am I supposed to study for two hours or ten hours for this test?"

"I need to go to class and try to pay attention no matter how boring the class is because that's what all of the good students do."

"I need to make sure I do the best I can because it's a privilege to be at this school."

"I need to do well because Mom and Dad are paying a lot of money for me to be here."

I'm sure these types of thoughts run through your head, and these are all valid concerns. The problem is, while you run around trying to please everyone else, you might end up forgetting that you also need to think about what's going to make you happy. Without coming up with your own ideas on how to approach schoolwork, you're just going to float around, approaching things the way other people think you should approach them. That's no fun.

It's true, you should consider everyone else, but if you can do it in a way that also takes care of your own personal needs, then it's going to be a lot easier on you and a lot better for you. If you spend your life trying to please the rest of the world and doing it "their way," life is going to be full of stress. And Lord knows you don't need another reason to run to that fifth of Captain Morgan.

All we're going to do for the rest of this chapter is list out the "other players'" agendas, and how their opinions and motives can influence you. As I run through this stuff, I want you to think about situations where you've had to deal with what I'm talking about. We'll go over how to tweak your approach toward dealing with the "other players" so that you can make thing easier on yourself.

In the next chapter, we'll shift the focus to **you**, and I'll help you develop your own personalized agenda. By the end of this section, you'll have a plan in place to get school done on your own terms, and you'll end up saving hours per week that you used to end up wasting when you were playing by everyone else's rules.

The Other Players

The University

Since universities are learning institutions, they're typically viewed as organizations that exist for the greater good of society. But, with the exception of a few institutions that are non-profits, make no mistake about it – the university's objective is to make money. How do they make money? For one, they get grants and donations, which oftentimes are based on their reputation and status. They also make their money on tuition, which... yep, you guessed it, is also directly correlated to their status and reputation.

Harvard has every single kid in America knocking down their doors to pay 50 grand a year to go to their school. Talk about a good business model! Since their objective is to have a good reputation, they need to make sure their graduates aren't a bunch of morons who misrepresent the school when they get out into the workforce.

If you run into some guy at your job who can't even tie his own shoelaces, and word gets out that he went to the University of Bros, you'd probably come to the conclusion that people from University of Bros are idiots. So, to combat this, the university will often force departments to have a certain curve in their class where only the best students get good grades.

This is a win-win situation for the university. Only the smartest kids will pass. Then, as an added bonus, they can stick the other kids who didn't pass with another semester's worth of tuition until they get through.

"But, what happens if I continually don't pass?"

Well, in the words of the great Kenny Powers, "You're fuckin' out!"

How do you like that? This is one of the only businesses in America that acts like you (the customer) are having a favor done for them by giving money to the business (the university.) Then, after they take your money, they can throw you out and ruin your reputation if they don't like your work, while making you seem like a degenerate who deserved it at the same time.

I'm sure you knew all of this before picking up this book. The reason I'm laying it out right now is so that you can realize that in a lot of instances, the university is a business, and you can't count on them to be a friend that will help you out when you need it. Instead, you'd be better off making it your job to make sure you know the rules of the university, and to constantly be on top of where you stand with them. **Treat the university as a competitor.**

You can even turn it into a game. You're here for the next four years. On one end, we've got you, whose goal is to graduate with good grades. On the other hand, we've got the university, whose goal is to get money from you. They'll set up road blocks like a crazy curve system, a minimum GPA to maintain while you're enrolled, and course requirements that are boring as hell. **You win the game** by jumping through their hoops and giving them what they want by meeting these requirements. **You win your game** by doing this on your own terms, with as little effort as possible, so you can spend your college time enjoying the "experience" that they advertise in the movies and on TV.

Keep the university and their agenda in the back of your head. Take care of them by giving them what they want. After that, you don't have to worry about them anymore. You have to play their game – that's a fact. But you **can** cut numerous corners so it really does feel like a game instead of a constant struggle.

The Professor

Professors are controlled by the university that writes their paychecks. They're forced in most instances to use the curve system and to make classes pretty difficult. Above all else, their objective is to keep their jobs.

There are good professors out there. If you've got a professor who cares about her students, puts in the effort to actually teach the material properly, and goes the extra mile to help you with your education, consider yourself lucky. Of course, the rest of the advice in this book is still applicable to your studies, but you'll just want to tune me out from time to time when I go off on the standard, by-the-book, paper-pushing douchebag professors that most students have to deal with in college. This book was not written to insult the good guys.

Now that we've cleared that up, let's talk about the douchebags. When a professor tries to put the minimum amount of effort in when it comes to dealing with their students, then that's a pretty good sign that they're a douchebag. They'll achieve this by establishing arbitrary, bureaucratic policies in the syllabus that leave little room for negotiation.

For your own benefit, you should shift your attitude when it comes to douchey professors. Instead of considering them as people to be respected and revered, treat them as an inanimate obstacle that is standing between you and your grade. It might sound cold, but if you create a distant attitude between yourself and these professors, you'll be a lot better off than if you sit around worrying about the professors' feelings all day, giving a damn about what they think of you.

The bottom line is, they determine whether or not you get a good grade. If you look at the big picture, their judgment could impact whether or not you're successful after you get out of school. If a certain assignment didn't get counted, and they won't change your grade, are you going to let the fact that "they're really a nice person" be enough of a reason not to cause a stink? Are you going to get a "C" as your final grade in a class you worked your ass off in, just because you're a respectful person who doesn't like to question authority? You shouldn't. Go hard on them, and fight for the grade you deserve.

At almost every university in the country, you'll be in situations more often than not where no one's looking out for you but yourself. These guys will not help you out and give you an extra point on a paper even if it was a mistake on their part that brought your grade down in the first place. Because of this, you've got to assume that there is absolutely no room for generosity or potential error on tests and assignments. Make sure that you dot all of your i's and cross of all your t's, so they can't take anything from you. Don't worry, we'll spend a big chunk of the rest of this book going through how to do this, and how to ensure you come out ahead over the professor and the university.

Your Peers

Well, they're just like you. They're shooting in the dark, trying to figure out the right things to do, and they're your competition in a sense when you're on the curve system. In everyone's quest to figure out how to pimp the system and get the best grades, you'll hear all sorts of nonsense and worried thoughts from your classmates. Mainly, you'll hear a bunch of crazy talk like, "Shit, I studied for eight hours for the short quiz last night. I hope I do all right," or, "I read the optional textbook from cover to cover too, even though the professor never mentioned anything about that being on the test." Meanwhile, you find yourself sitting next to these guys and getting worried because you only studied for an hour and you thought that was too much.

Don't let these guys get into your head. It would be like taking stock market advice from some homeless guy lying around outside of a 7-Eleven. Unfortunately, the lack of information out there on how to study properly creates all of this madness and confusion. To remedy this, all you have to do is stay in your own lane.

A fascinating aspect of the human mind is that we tend to think about what other people think. Then, without noticing it, oftentimes we assume that our opinions of other people's opinions are really the truth. Over time, you end up with an accumulation of a bunch of concepts in your head that you think are true, when really, they never had any basis in reality in the first place.

"Who gives a shit, and how does this apply to me doing better in college?"

Great question.

Let's pretend for a second that I'm a freshman in college and I'm trying to figure out the grand answer of how to be a better student. There's some guy in my Anthropology class named Sean who just seems like he's really smart. He's got glasses, he's really nerdy looking, and he always answers questions during class. Instead of paying attention to what the professor is saying during class, my mind starts thinking about how smart this Sean guy is, and what he probably does to study for tests.

For some reason, the next thing I think of is how this Sean guy looks sort of like one of these kids I saw four years ago in a segment on *20/20* that focused on rich high school students from New York City. These kids would get together at coffee shops and hire a keynote speaker from the field that they're studying, and the guy would come in and teach them one-on-one about the subject before their test. After these special studying sessions, the kids would end up acing their tests.

Without thinking about the fact that these kids scored well on their tests because they were taught by an expert from the field that they were studying, I think to myself, "I bet Sean probably studies in coffee shops too. Hmm, maybe that's the key to getting my studying right!"

So now, I've got two unproven and baseless assumptions in my head.

Baseless Assumption #1) This Sean guy is smart.

Baseless Assumption #2) Coffee shops are good for studying.

But I never realize that these assumptions are based on nothing. I go on with my life, and a month later, I tell my friend Adam that I'm going to study in a coffee shop because I think it will improve my grades. He tells his little sister Melissa about that, and before you know it, her entire high school starts studying at coffee shops.

I get a "D" on my next test because I was paying more attention to which type of milk I should get in my latte than I was to the wonders of Anthropology. Meanwhile, Sean is found dead in the subway station two weeks later after a high-stakes shootout with Colombian drug lords.

Obviously, that's a sarcastic example that was blown out of proportion, but do you see where I'm going with this here? Your mind can turn fiction into an assumed reality. Worse yet, a lot of the advice you're getting from your peers is not even "real" advice that actually works. It's just their own fiction that they assume is true. So, unless you know another student who gets good grades and has approaches and techniques that work for them with proven results (the results being – they get "A's,") then take your classmates' advice with a grain of salt. A lot of it is a bunch of convoluted horseshit.

A Good Way to Tell if You're Dealing With Clueless People

I'm sure you've dealt with morons at customer service centers over the phone before. You know the drill. You buy airfare online, and then you have a question as to if the flight you purchased is transferable. The website gives a generic answer with no real solution. On your quest to find a real answer, you wind up on the phone with someone from the Philippines, and guess what they tell you? That same goddamn answer you saw on the website, word for word.

If you ask them a real question that requires knowledge about the policy on this matter, they'll either just recite the same answer again, or they might even just lie and say, "Oh yeah, it is transferable." But, the key point is, you can tell in the tone of their voice when they lie that they have no idea what the fuck they're talking about.

This is the same routine and generic attitude that will be present in your peers when they have no clue what's going on in school. If you keep hearing the same words from your friends that don't make sense and that you've already read in the textbook, with no real passion or clarity coming from their mouths, then they can't be relied on as a viable source of information.

Don't put it past some of these people to really commit to the fact that they "know it all." Some of these guys need to feel like they're always a part of the in-crowd, even when they're not. After about a week of being more observant of what I described here, you'll be able to spot these clowns like a senior citizen at a Kanye West concert.

Your Parents

I'm sure your parents just want you to do well and are generally on your side. But it's worth noting here that they can often expect you to turn water into wine. You know the comments...

"You have a 'C' right now. Why can't you just do better?"

"I don't care if the professor won't change your grade, even though it was their fault and they misplaced your homework assignment. You need that grade bumped up to an 'A.'"

These criticisms are just sources of unnecessary stress. You can't change things that are impossible, and you know that. So it's best to just leave it at that instead of arguing with them, or, worse yet, beating yourself up about it.

Parents have an added interest in your education, because in a lot of cases, they're paying for it! Again, it's understandable that they want to make sure you're doing fine, and in almost every case, they want you to do well because they love you. So do yourself **and them** a favor and give them a break. Even if they don't understand how hard it is to be a college student and to master this art of getting good grades, it's at least kind of nice that they care enough to be in your business about it.

Since you love them and don't want to fight with them, but you might not be able to stand their constant assessment of your life, the real objective here is to get relief from the pressure and to get them off your back without turning this into a whole bunch of drama.

Here's how you achieve this. All you have to do is simply take their advice, and tell them what they want to hear. Tell them how much you've studied and how seriously you take school. But if they expect you to be studying for eight hours when you only need one, then you can always just lie about it. I'm not endorsing this if you have a moral objection toward it. But if all it takes is to say, "Oh yeah, I studied a whole bunch," to get them to shut up and for you to be able to handle things your way, then everyone wins.

You're not going to win if you try to change their views or get into an argument with them about the amount of effort you're putting in. Just tell them what they want to hear, but then do whatever the hell you want to. Try this out, and see how it works.

CHAPTER 2

Four Life-Changing Concepts to Start With Right Away

After all we just went through, doesn't this whole school thing seem almost like one big guessing game?

"Am I going to get an 'A' if I study the textbook and the study guide, or do I need to consult outside sources too?"

"If I mess up my Spanish test, I'm never going to hear the end of it from Mom."

"Should I study with my friend Brad? Even though I would do better if I studied on my own, I know he needs help."

"You know what? Fuck Brad. That dude still owes me ten bucks."

For a second here, let's throw everyone else's agendas and opinions out the window so we can focus on **you**.

How are you going to change your approach to school? Well, we first need to start with establishing an objective of what you want out of your academic experience.

Are you here just to collect a degree and do as little work as possible, no matter what classes you're taking?

Maybe you're just looking for a way to minimize the amount of time you put in to boring classes you don't care about, but still spend the majority of your time learning in other classes that interest you?

Or, are you just interested in playing by the rules? You're fine with the normal way of doing school, and you picked up this book to improve your school skills, but not to save time by finding ways to pimp the system.

If you want to follow the rules, feel free to skip the rest of this section. But, assuming that you're interested in approaching school in a new way and saving time during boring classes, let's establish what you can do to reshape your college experience.

The rest of this chapter will introduce you to four life-changing concepts. Once you get acquainted with them, you'll learn how to think like a time-efficient master, and you'll be well on your way toward success.

By the way, I don't want you to follow my advice blindly throughout the course of this book. If you disagree with my opinions, the methods I present, or any comments that I make, then, by all means, disregard them and do it your own way instead.

Life Changing Concept # 1 – First Define What's Going to Make You Successful

There's plenty of ways to define success. In the business world, success is normally defined by profit. But what defines a successful school experience? That's something that's unique to everyone, and it's something that you need to figure out for yourself.

Some people might say their success in school is defined by their grade point average. That's a good start. But what else is it going to take for you to become "successful" in college? You'll only view yourself as successful in college if you accomplish the things that you want to accomplish.

Maybe you'll define your college experience as successful only if you join a fraternity or sorority and go to parties three times a week.

Maybe it's all about scoring internships for you, and if you come out of college without work experience, then your whole time in school is a bust.

Maybe you define success as being able to get good grades while still having a life at the same time.

Whatever you want out of college, take the time to write it down now. It won't take you long to do this. Think about it, and think big.

If you want to find your future husband during college and that's the real objective here, then let that be the star of the show. Make that your number one priority during your "college experience." Don't bullshit around and go to an extra credit lecture for Biology when you could be going out on a date. You need to do what matters to you. When you specifically decide what you want, you'll stop wasting time doing things you don't want to do.

Now, obviously, this book isn't going to teach you how to find your soul mate, or how to pull off Edward 40-Hands without throwing up. This book is here to help you with school-related activities and to make them as little of a hassle as possible, so you can then spend more time pursuing your social/career/life goals. Now that you've recognized what you really want, it's time to minimize some of the boring aspects of school so you can spend your time pursuing what you want. Let's talk about how to make that happen.

Life Changing Concept #2 – Plan Ahead

Planning ahead might sound like a basic concept, but if you apply it right, the potential power of this concept can be huge.

If you're going to be this bad ass schoolwork assassin like I'm training you to become, make no mistake about it – you can't be lazy. You may confuse some of this stuff as laziness because the emphasis is on putting as little effort in as possible where it's not needed. But don't get it twisted. It's really about putting in 110% in the right places so you can then fuck around and watch TV all day while you're hungover. Think of it as being efficient for the purpose of being lazy later.

Being successful in college can be achieved by applying yourself in a smart way. But remember, trying to apply yourself in ways that your professor, your parents, and your peers think you should, but you disagree with, will just cause you to waste time and give up freedom in your own life. Be smart, and apply yourself in ways that you think are right.

Picking Classes

I'm sure most of you have heard of the website RateMyProfessors.com. It's a site where students can log on and post comments about their past professors. The comments can range from, "Damn, this teacher was hot," to, "Make sure to buy the optional textbook that's suggested on the syllabus because the test questions are straight out of that book."

Needless to say, this place is a goldmine, not only for finding hints and tips about what to expect from your class and what to study, but, most of all, for finding out which professors you should sign up with in the first place.

Here, before the semester even begins, you need to start your plan of attack. You can start by looking at the classes that you're going to have to take. You probably know off the top of your head which ones are going to be extremely boring. So let's say you have to take Geology 101. Unless you're a rock scholar, this is a class where you want to get in, get done, and get the fuck out.

Log onto RateMyProfessors.com and look up the names of all the professors teaching the class. Read all of the comments. In most instances, you'll be able to learn if the professor is a hard ass or not, if attendance is required, if a paper or homework is assigned, and if the tests are straight out of the book.

The more "by the book," the better. If this guy gives three midterms, all based on the textbook, with no homework or papers, this is the person you need to sign up for.

Don't worry about if the other students say he's boring, because you won't be going to the class much anyway.

Don't worry if the class is scheduled for Tuesday nights and you don't like night classes, **because you won't be going to the class much anyway** (see Life Changing Concept #3 for that.)

Always sign up for the easiest professor if you're taking a class that you could care less about. Don't be fooled by your own optimistic side, which might say:

"Well, even though I'll have to write a couple of extra papers and do weekly assignments with this professor, maybe this guy can make Geology fun and I'll actually develop an interest in it."

I've never met anyone who has been happy after making a decision like that. Maybe you're in the 5% that that works for, and if you are, then by all means, go for it. But, if you're trying to make things easy on yourself, then be smart about this and choose the path of least resistance.

Here's some more advice about RateMyProfessors. If a professor has no reviews posted about her, or only a couple, she may be a new professor. If this is the case, it's a crapshoot. She could be easy, or she could be terrible. My advice would be to avoid her, and instead go for the proven commodities. The more reviews, the better.

Also, double check that the review you're reading is actually for your specific class. Professors will often teach, for instance, both Geology 101 and Geology 104. If you're taking Geology 101, the 104 reviews are irrelevant, other than general comments about the professor's disposition and the class environment. Don't base your decision on those reviews. You need reviews about the specific class you're taking.

Your Class Schedule

Here's where a lot of people drop the ball. It always seems super convenient before the semester or quarter starts and you have this perfect lineup of five classes on Monday Wednesday and Friday with an hour carved out for lunch. If you can get this lineup with the classes that you want, that's amazing. But don't give up the easy, slam-dunk classes so you can have a more fluid schedule. Trust me, you will regret it.

If you sign up for the dick who fails 60% of students for Accounting 202 just because the class neatly tucks into your schedule at 1:45 on Wednesdays, you're going to waste 30 extra hours fighting for your life during the semester, and you're going to be way more stressed out the entire time. It's not worth it in most cases. You've done the research. If the professor is bad news, stay the hell away from him.

Plus, your class schedule is pretty irrelevant anyway. For classes that you want to actually enjoy and participate in, then it does matter when they occur. However, for these throwaway classes, you can count on showing up to them as little as five or six times a semester.

"Oh God," you may be thinking. *"Are you saying that I should start skipping class? That's going to be a guaranteed failure."*

Not if you adopt the right mind-set...

Life Changing Concept #3 – For Every Throwaway Class, Focus on Your Grade, and Nothing Else

For focused success when it comes to getting through a boring class, all you need to do is care about your **grade** and nothing else. That's the only rule you have to remember.

"Well no shit, dumbass. I've always cared about my grade. So what are you saying?"

I'm saying that a subtle change in your focus and thinking will completely reshape the way you approach these classes. It'll turn you into a zoned-in class-ripping warrior who spends about 10% of the effort, while getting better results, than the overachiever blowhards do.

Let me say it again. Care about **your grade** before anything else. That means that all you need to be thinking about is, "How do I get an 'A' in this class?" That's your number one, and only objective. Nothing else matters.

Do you need to show up to class if the tests are straight out of the book? Maybe not.

Do you need to attend optional lectures, just to score "brownie points" with your professor, even though there's no room for subjective grading in your class? Hell no.

As long as you focus on exactly what you need to do to get an "A" in the class, then the other requirements that you feel you had to do because they made you a "good student" can be dropped entirely. Instead of showing up to class even though you never end up learning anything from the professor, or going to all-night study sessions in the library with your friends where you just end up watching re-runs of *It's Always Sunny In Philadelphia* on a laptop, you can be in bed sleeping, out at a party, or shopping.

In Class

How many times have you shown up to a class and fallen asleep? How many times have you actually paid attention? Personally, my mind would wander in class unless the professor's teaching style were especially captivating. If you're stuck in a shit class like this, then it's time to reassess if you really want to be there or not.

The first question you need to ask yourself is:

"Am I realistically going to be able to pay attention or not?"

The question isn't:

"Do I want to be a good student and pay attention?"

Of course you **want** to be a good student. But again, let's be honest here. If you're coming into your Calculus class and **trying** to pay attention, but, after five minutes, you just can't take it and start spacing out, then you're not **going** to be able to pay attention. It's definitely fair to give it a shot for a couple weeks and see if things get better. But if they don't improve, and you sit through the class like a zombie, it's time to cut your losses.

Your time could be just as well spent swimming laps in a pool or starting an eBay business. You're not doing yourself any good by sitting through the class, and all you're doing is flushing three to five hours a week of your time right down the shitter. I don't know about you, but there are few feelings as unpleasant as sitting in a crowded classroom when you just can't pay attention. I imagine it's similar to what sitting in a jail cell feels like, except you have the added stress of keeping your appearance up to make it look like you give half of a shit so you don't get called out by the professor.

The point is – if the teaching style isn't working for you, you're going to need to find another way to learn the material. Going to the class and staring at a blank wall isn't the way to do it.

The good news is, if you did your research and picked the right professor, hopefully you're in a class where the tests are all based on what's in the textbook. If you're sitting through one of the lectures, and you realize that your douchebag professor is just reciting the same definition off a PowerPoint slide that you've already seen word for word in your textbook, then you're in great shape. This essentially means that attending these lectures is useless, as long as you study the textbook.

But even if that's not the case, and you just can't stop yourself from falling asleep, you've got to confront the reality that you're not going to pay attention. If you don't learn the material in class, you're going to have to buy other books on the topic, talk with friends that had the class before to find out what's on the tests, or read the textbook yourself and decide what you need to study from there. That's going to take time, so you don't want to waste your week dicking around in class for no reason. **Don't go to the class.** You're doing nothing for yourself.

Think about all of the time you'll immediately save, and how much more efficient you'll become. You can skip the five hours of worthless time in class, and spend one focused hour reading the textbook - an hour that you wouldn't have spent in the past because your schedule was so crowded when you were forcing yourself to attend class. You would have been lost in regards to the test material with the old routine, but with the new routine, in 20% of the time, you're actually learning.

Sometimes, you'll get screwed, and the professor will institute a mandatory attendance policy. If this is the case, you're in a tough spot. There were a few times in my college years where I just forfeited the 10% of my grade for the mandatory attendance and went about my business. But, sometimes they'll pull some other stunt where they say something like, "If you miss more than four classes, then the highest grade you can get in the class is a D." Bastards.

If you're stuck in a class for this reason, I suggest reading Chapter 16, "Fun Games to Play During Class," to keep yourself sane during these boring lectures. Also, if you're going to be stuck in the class, I'd recommend bringing any sort of studying material that you need to get done anyway, and work on it during the lecture instead of listening to the professor. It's easy enough to tune them out, and if you're reading the textbook for your own class, there's no way the professor can call you out for not paying attention.

If you're free to attend the class as you choose, I'd recommend thinking about your options here if you don't enjoy the class or can't pay attention.

I know so many people who have a big aversion to skipping class. It might just be the general fear of doing something out of the ordinary that goes against the rules. A lot of times they say they're worried that they're going to miss something important on the test. Well, even if you miss one or two "test questions" during the class, isn't it worth getting two questions wrong on a test of 50 questions instead of spending up to 75 hours of your life during the class doing nothing? The answer is obvious.

When Should I Show Up to Class?

Obviously, you need to show up to class a few times a semester so that you can have a general idea of what's going on. You need to know what to study for when you sit down on your own and try to learn the material. If you have reliable friends in the class that attend the lectures regularly, you can get the information from them and save yourself the trip. But, if you're flying solo here, I'd recommend showing up at least once every two weeks just to keep tabs on the direction of the class and to make sure that the professor is following what's been outlined in the syllabus. As long as you know what's going to be on the tests, and you feel like you have a handle on what's been going on during the lectures while you're gone, then you're in good shape.

The best time to show up to class is during the last couple of lectures before a midterm. Chances are, you'll actually get a review of material relevant for the test presented to you. Who cares about learning something if it's **not** relevant to the test? Remember, if it's not going to help your grade, then it doesn't matter to you anymore. There's no better time to get the material you need for the test than during these "study guide review lectures."

Before a test, professors may give you a study guide, reminding you of all of the key points covered in class that might show up on the test. In other words, they basically hand you the test before they administer it. How could it get any easier?

During the lecture, the professor may run through each concept on the study guide, giving you a breakdown of each term. If he does this, you're in luck, because everything will be laid out completely for you. The crucial thing to remember here while you're taking notes is to write everything down **exactly how the professor says it.** You can also write a quick definition in "your own words" later beside it, but focus on writing down every single word he says first.

You want to preserve his phrasings, because nine times out of ten, that exact same phrasing will show up on the test. If you keep reviewing a certain sentence that was written in the professor's wording over and over again during your studying, you'll be able to pick it out right away during the test. We'll talk about how to utilize these notes to a big extent in Section 3. Until then, file this into the back of your mind.

If the professor doesn't go over specific terminology from the study guide to your liking, there should be time for questions at the end of the lecture, and you better start asking some. Don't worry about the fact that you weren't in attendance when these concepts were explained the first time around, and that you really have no idea what the fuck is going on at this point. Nod your head when they ask, "Remember when we talked about **this?**" and keep asking for clarification. They may assume you're just a dumbass, or they may realize you didn't attend the class. Either way, it doesn't matter. Remember, if your grade is based on the tests only, there's no room for your professor to screw you on anything else, no matter how big of an asshole he thinks you are.

Also feel free to go to his office hours to get more answers filled in on your study guide. Keep in mind that some professors aren't always going to be happy about being bothered during office hours, even though they're required by the university to hold them in the first place. Just milk them for all they're worth, and keep it moving.

Life-Changing Concept #4: Relax and Have a Life

After you're done with whatever it is that you need to do to meet your objective (by the way…what's your objective again? – to get an "A" in the class!) then it's time to leave the bullshit at the door and have some fun. You need to find a way to get out of the grind of constant scrambling and school stress if you're serious about enjoying your college experience. School shouldn't be on your mind 24/7.

Think about it for a second. You might put an emphasis on your physical fitness by making it a point to go to the gym three times a week. But I bet the next time you're hanging out with your friends, you're not thinking about the fact that you're going to be running on the treadmill tomorrow. You just go to the gym, do your workout, and you're done. The same type of mentality can also be applied to schoolwork.

There's only a finite amount of work that can be done in school. After you've made a decision on how to approach your class schedule (i.e. – "I'm going to skip Geology this week, but I'll definitely go to my Psychology class because I think it's interesting,") then it's time to relax about it. You don't need to invest anything else emotionally into Geology, or really even think about it anymore. All you need to do is make sure you're able to score well on the tests by following whatever plan you came up with.

If you have legitimate work to do, like if it's time to grind out a paper or study for the test, your life still doesn't need to be a bundle of stress. Remember, there's only a finite amount of work to be done. After you're finished, it's time to move on to your personal life and let go of the school world.

Have you ever been on vacation and realized after a few days that you're so much more relaxed? You don't have that constant nagging feeling that you have to be doing something, and the freedom from that alone makes things so much more enjoyable.

You might not be able to feel completely free all of the time. But, if you take a more matter-of-fact approach to your schoolwork, you'll actually have more fun when you're doing the things you want to, like going out with your friends, hitting up dances, and drinking.

Even if you live on campus and you're constantly reminded of the work that you have to do, there's definitely ways to free yourself from this stress. You need to put an emphasis on decreasing your stress level. Scientifically speaking, stress will actually make you physically tired.

You always hear people with 9 to 5 jobs saying, "I don't take my work home with me." For some reason, no one feels like the college demographic deserves that same relief. School, and all the crap associated with it, is extremely stressful. It's more stressful in many instances than a job in the "real world." But, in our society, you've been trained to belittle yourself by saying, "Oh, I'm just a student."

You deserve to relax.

An easy way to take a break is to find some spots outside of the campus area where college people don't hang out. You might just need to find a movie theater 20 minutes away from the action to decompress every so often. Having even a couple hours a week away from the madness can do wonders for your stress level and your overall well-being.

After a while, you'll treat the "school and grades" part of school as an easy-to-do chore that you can take care of when you need to take care of it. The rest of the time, your mind will automatically think about other things.

If you're done for the day, but everyone else around you is still running around like chickens with their heads cut off, don't sweat it either. This is the beauty of doing things your way, and knowing that you can rely on yourself. You've got it down. Other people are going to continue to overstress and overextend themselves. Just focus on yourself. Do your work, do it efficiently, and do it on your own schedule. That's all you have to worry about.

Section 2: Assignments

CHAPTER 3

Polishing Your Grammar Skills

It's time to discuss writing. Now, I know there are probably two groups of people reading this right now. One group is saying, "Oh yeah, writing's not that big of a deal for me. I'd rather write a paper than take a test." The other group is saying, "Fuck me. I hate writing. I'm a terrible writer." The next four chapters are for that second group.

You're Never Going to Mess Up Your Words Again

You want to seem like an intelligent person when you're writing, and there's no greater red flag to a professor, or anyone else who's educated, when they see you misusing the words we're about to cover in this chapter.

Now, if you don't know the correct way to use these words currently, it doesn't actually mean that you're an idiot or that you're uneducated. It simply means that you never learned these really quick and easy rules. I can't stress this enough though – when you fuck these things up, it stings people who understand the rules, and you're almost automatically written off as a low-class moron, or, at an absolute minimum, someone who didn't proofread his or her own paper.

In our text-message-heavy generation, a lot of the rules on these words have been ignored and sometimes even get a, "Oh yeah, I might know the rules, but who gives a shit anyway?" type-attitude taken toward them. Trust me, anyone middle-aged and older gives a shit, and they're going to be the ones grading your paper. You need to get these right every time.

If you get confused by grammar terms like "possessive," "plural," and "singular" while reading this section, don't waste your time trying to figure them out. I've included examples after the definitions, so you'll be able to understand how to use each word anyway. Read this section slowly, because it gets a little tricky unless you're really paying attention.

Your vs. You're

Your – The possessive form of "you."

Examples:

"Is this your shirt?"
"Can I borrow your copy of *Scarface* on Blu-ray?"
"Your eyes are beautiful, hottie."

You're – A contraction (hence the apostrophe) for "you are."

Examples:

"You're sexy."
"Let me know if you're going to come with me to the Katy Perry concert next week."

"You're a real asshole."

If you can substitute the words "you are" in the sentence that you are writing, then you should use "you're." If not, it's always going to be "your." Remembering that makes it easy.

It's vs. Its

This is a weird one, and it's counterintuitive.

It's – A contraction for "it is." That's it.

Examples:

"It's really important to me that you come to my birthday party."
"It's the third week of March."
"It's fucking impossible for me to understand all this shit."

Its – The possessive form of "it." You can also remember it as any other instance of "its," besides when you can substitute the word for "it is."

Examples:

"Cute dog. What's its name?"
"That fly is annoying. I'm going to end its life!"

Normally, we're used to putting an apostrophe at the end of a possessive word. For example, you might say, "Where are Joe's sunglasses?" This is where most people screw up with "its." You would think that when you're referring to a dog, you might say, "Should I get it's leash?" because the leash you're referring to belongs to the dog. But because everyone already uses the "it's" with an apostrophe as a contraction for "it is," whoever wrote the rules on the English language decided that we shouldn't put an apostrophe in when something is possessive here. It sucks, but get used to it.

Who's vs. Whose

This one is similar to "Its vs. It's."

Who's – Like "it's," this is the contraction for "Who is." Again, ask yourself, "Can I substitute 'who is' in the sentence I'm writing?" If the answer is yes, then you should use "who's." That's the only time you'll use this.

Examples:

"Who's that sexy beast over there?"
"Dr. Gardener is the prick who's responsible for my botched plastic surgery."

Whose – This is the possessive form of "who."

Examples:

"The artist in question is Ke$ha, whose debut album *Animal* was certified platinum by the RIAA in 2010."
"Whose shoes are these?"
"There's one individual here tonight whose confidence has transcended beyond what I could have ever imagined. The 'Most Improved Award' goes to Rebecca."

This one will get confusing in instances like the plastic surgeon example, where it almost feels natural to put "whose." But remember, if you can substitute the word for "who is," then it's "who's."

You wouldn't put "The artist in question is Ke$ha, **who is** debut album…" That doesn't make any sense. That's what "whose" is for.

Their, They're, and There

Their – Referring to something that someone possesses.

Examples:

"I want to go over to their house next Tuesday."
"That teddy bear is theirs."

They're – A contraction for "They are."

Examples:

"They're coming over in an hour."
"They're the nicest people I know."

There – Any other instance of the word. It's most typically used in reference to direction, but there's many other ways to use it.

Examples:

"Go pick up my ball over there."
"Rachel's right there."
"There was a time when I really didn't care about the world."
"See what I mean? There, you got it!"

Since there are three different forms of this word, it's best to just memorize when to use each instance. If it helps, you can always check to see if "they're" is appropriate to use by substituting it for "they are" in the sentence you're trying to write.

To vs. Too

To – Referring to direction, or used as a preposition.

Examples:

"I'm going to Portland in February."
"To many people, the economy is in a bad spot, but to me, it seems fine."

Too – Used in reference to description, or, a synonym for "also."

Examples in reference to description:
"That guy is too short for me to date."

"The movie was too boring to warrant a theatrical release."

Examples as a synonym for "also":
"Can Jessie come too?"
"I already have mustard on my burger, but I want ketchup now too!"

Than vs. Then

Than – Used only for comparison purposes.

Examples:

"My music collection is bigger than Justin's."
"I'd rather ride the subway than take a taxi."
"The love that I have for you is described by more than words."
"More often than not, you'll get the runs after eating at Sal's Pizza Parlor."

Then – Can be used to describe a point in time, or something that's going to occur next. It can also be used as a transition word like "therefore." Basically, all you need to remember is that "then" is what you'll use every time unless you're comparing things.

Examples:

"If you were going to show up to my house drunk, then why didn't you do it with a little class?"
"If he yells at me one more time, then I'm going over there to knock his ass out."
"I went out to dinner with Christine, then to the movies."
"You want to meet up at 6? I'll see you then."

Weather vs. Whether

This one isn't as easily confused, but here's the difference:

Weather – The physical climate outside, or describing someone or something which has endured hardship or constant exposure.

Examples:

"The weather is terrible today."
"My wallet has a real weathered look to it after constant use for five years."

Whether – In reference to choosing between two things.

Examples:

"I need to pick whether I'm going to drink hard liquor or beer tonight."
"Whether or not you come on this trip, Jim, I'll still be your friend."
"Whether short or tall, I love you all."

Farther vs. Further

Farther – In reference to actual, physical distance.

Examples:

"I'm going to walk farther than you during the hike today."
"I can throw the ball farther than Sammy."

Further – In reference to theoretical, figurative distance.

Examples:

"The further you develop your mind, the more competent you will become."
"I just called you a bitch. Do I need to explain that I hate you any further?"

This one is confused by most people, including some professors. You'll be ahead of the game if you know this difference.

Getting Apostrophes Right

Apostrophes can be confusing as hell at times. Sometimes people like to throw an apostrophe in just because something is plural. For instance, in that sentence above, if I were doing things incorrectly, I might say, "apostrophe's can be confusing as hell at times." You might see "Spaghetti and Meatball's" or "Burger's" on a menu, or your favorite bar offering "Karaoke Thursday's." This is all wrong.

An apostrophe should only occur in two instances — in reference to possession, or in a contraction. Sure, you can also include an apostrophe if you're talking about a single letter and you don't want the plural form to get confused for another word, like "Getting A's" as opposed to "Getting As." But don't worry about that. Here are a few examples of where you'll run into the apostrophe 95% of the time…

Possessive Apostrophe:

"Can I borrow Olivia's book for tomorrow?"
"Kelly's ass is just out of this world."
"Tom's weed stash is the best on campus."

Contraction Apostrophe:

"What's your phone number?"
Short for: "What is your phone number?"
"Why's everybody yelling at me today?"
Short for: "Why is everybody yelling at me today?"
"They've set me up with the Feds."
Short for: "They have set me up with the Feds."

Now, apostrophes can get more complicated when there's more than one person involved in the sentence. If the word you're using is a reference to a group, then it will always be the word, followed by an apostrophe, followed by an "S."

Examples:

"Where is the gentlemen's bathroom?"
"Who cares about other people's opinions?"

Since "gentlemen" and "people" are already plural words, you just need to add the apostrophe and then the "S."

Now, let's talk about using the plural form of a normally singular word. For instance, if you were talking about using the pool at the Johnson house, then you would refer to the family as "The Johnsons." The Johnsons, since you're talking about the whole family, are now a plural reference, so you add an "S" on their name. Now, to talk about using their pool, this is how you would write it:

"I used the Johnsons' pool last night."

Do you get it? It's the same as saying something about a singular person like we did above…

Earlier Example:

"Kelly's ass is just out of this world."

…but since we already added the extra "S" on the Johnson family name to make it plural, we don't put another "S" on the end after the apostrophe. Here's another example:

"That swindler stole all of the employees' pensions."

If we were talking about one employee, it would be "the employee's pension," but since we're talking about a group, we include an "S" on the end of the root word, and then leave the second "S" off.

When writing a word that ends in an "S" even when it's singular that **also** requires an apostrophe, it's debatable what you should do. The rules are unclear, and the accepted format keeps changing. The bottom line is, either one of the following forms are acceptable, and you're not going to get marked down either way, because there is no clear, golden standard at this time.

Example with an extra S: "I hooked up with James's ex-girlfriend last night."
Also acceptable: "I hooked up with James' ex-girlfriend last night."

All of this stuff is arbitrary. It doesn't always make sense. And of course, it's not acceptable to hook up with James' ex-girlfriend. But, these are the rules. So just remember this stuff, reference this chapter if you need help, and make sure you get it right when you're writing for class.

CHAPTER 4

Step Up Your Vocab

As you can tell by now, I'm not going to encourage you to go out and do more work. The emphasis of this book is on doing the least amount of work possible, for maximum results. If I told you to go out, pick up a thesaurus and start memorizing words, what would I look like? There's a better, easier, and more relevant way to develop your vocabulary. All you need to do is look out for new vocabulary words in your everyday life.

You know the drill. That scholarly cousin of yours drones on over a family dinner about politics. You normally just tune him out because he sounds like a douche. This time, pay attention. Don't pay attention to the content of what he's saying, but just listen for a few words he uses that you didn't recognize. Make a note of the words. If you have a smartphone, use the Notes section. If you don't, just save a text message draft with the words in it.

Then, next time you've got a few extra minutes and Google at your fingertips, look the words up. You don't have to memorize them. That would be too much work. If the words are interesting enough to you, they will stick in your brain.

The same goes for class. If you happen to be in class, and you hear the professor using a word you don't know, then write that down too.

If you're reading an article in *Time* magazine and you see a word that you don't know, look it up.

Do it all the time. You can spend a grand total of about 10 minutes a week doing this, and over months of time, you'll have built up a pretty solid vocabulary.

This works because it's easy, but it's also cool because these words you're pulling out are actually relevant to the world around you. The articles you're reading, the classes you're taking, the people you hang out with – these words have been used around you. Why learn a random word out of the dictionary, when these words have actually been included in your everyday life, in one way or another?

CHAPTER 5

Ripping Up Papers – Writing 101

I'm Not a Natural Writer! Help!

Now that you've polished your grammar and vocabulary game, let's talk about the writing process. You might feel like you're no good at writing, and when you sit down to actually put words onto paper, you don't know where to start. Don't get down on yourself for that. I bet you've never thought about this, but you're already writing in a natural and free-flowing way every time you send a text or write an e-mail.

When you write an e-mail, or especially a text message, I doubt that you sit down to think about your writing. Those messages, especially the more conversational e-mails to a friend or family member, just come naturally. Check them out now. Read them for yourself. Even though they're not written the same way you would write a paper, it's a start.

The point is, you are a "natural writer" in some capacity, whether you realize it yet or not. You might just be stuck when it comes to writing a big college paper because you're scrambling around trying to figure out exactly what you should do. Well, the rest of this chapter will show you exactly what you should do once and for all, so you never have to worry about it again.

When writing a paper, you'll need to turn in a piece of work that has some substance to it if you're expecting to get a good grade. To make things easy on you, I've laid out five key ingredients that you should include in your paper to make it great. As long as you have all five of these elements working together within your paper, you'll undoubtedly improve your grade. We'll go over each ingredient in further detail as the chapter progresses.

The Five Key Ingredients for a Great Paper

☑ **Ingredient #1: Throw in "Key Terms"**
Include the terms and key buzz words that the professor wants to hear.

☑ **Ingredient #2: Give Them a Demonstration**
Show the professor that you can define these terms. Demonstrate that you know what you're talking about.

☑ **Ingredient #3: Use Your "Grandma Voice"**
Don't write the way you would normally speak in front of your friends while you're drafting up a paper. When you clean up your language, talk more formally, and speak in complete sentences, you're using your "Grandma Voice." Use this for your papers.

☑ **Ingredient #4: Add a Dash of Flair**
Come up with ideas, arguments, and conclusions for your paper that will show your professor that you're thinking outside the box. Put your creativity on full display, and don't be afraid to share unique ideas, as long as they're not too over-the-top.

☑ **Ingredient #5: Refine Your Wording**
Write in complete sentences, and make it sound like this paper was something that you were **inspired** to write. Make it seem like you actually thought about the creation of this paper and that it means something to you. Don't make it look like you just mechanically threw a bunch of scattered topics together.

Remember that every paper you write is simply **an assignment.** It doesn't need to be an esoteric piece of art that's impossible to create. The professor is looking for a few simple things here, and if you get them right, you'll get a good grade. Are you going to get 100% on the paper if you don't come up with an interesting conclusion that ties the whole thing together? Probably not. But if you're not there, and you at least show that you're trying, you'll still get a decent grade. You get a lot of points for just "showing up" and writing the thing. Never forget that.

Cover Your Bases

The most crucial elements of the paper are the first two ingredients. If your paper is based off of a prompt, at the risk of sounding redundant here, guess what? You have to answer the prompt! Don't dance around the meat and potatoes of the paper. Answer the damn questions.

Also be sure to include terms, topics, and "buzz words" that you've seen mentioned either in class or in the syllabus. Go the extra mile here and include a sentence defining or explaining these terms as well. It never hurts to do this, and it gives the professor no excuses to mark you down.

Think of these papers as mini-tests. The purpose isn't just to get you to write something - it's also to see if you understand the fundamentals of the class. The more opportunities that you have to demonstrate that you understand the material and the general take-home messages, the better.

Papers are easy points to drop in your bucket, because all of this stuff is done at home (and don't worry, I'll cover in-class essays in Section 4.) You have all of the resources in the world at home to do some research and produce sound definitions on these topics throughout the course of the paper. Don't be lazy.

Outline It

So, now that you know **what** to include for the first two ingredients of your paper, you need to lay out a plan for **how** it's going to be written. I would recommend writing an outline before you start writing your paper. Now, by outline, I don't mean the type of outline you're required to write as an assignment before a paper is due. When you're writing an outline just because it's an assignment you're forced to do, it turns into a waste of time. Outlines get a bad rap because you're used to writing them when you don't want to.

To use the power of the outline to your advantage, start by writing out all of the main points you're going to cover. This will probably take longer than you expect. You're actually going to have to sit down and think about your entire paper.

The purpose of writing the outline is **so that you can write the entire paper** without worrying about the exact words you're going to use. It's an incredibly liberating way to write.

Let's say that I was going to write a paper on the advantages of going to Taco Bell to eat. Inside of the outline, I would write my main points, and I would also include notes to myself on where to start with more elaborate ideas that I know would require further research or that would take too much time to flesh out right away. By doing it this way, I don't get caught up in the details, but I get everything laid out ahead of time.

My outline might look something like this:

Title - Taco Bell Paper (Final Title Pending)

- ☑ Intro – Say something profound about the fast food industry. Then list off all my main points. Then throw in a little preview of the conclusion that I'm going to bring in later.

- ☑ Point 1 – Fast food eateries are way cheaper to eat at than restaurants. I'll throw in some statistic I find online about how much cheaper (like 85%) fast food restaurants are than their restaurant counterparts. Then I'll say that you get a huge portion of food when considering that you're paying this little, and also throw in something else about free refills on drinks being an added bonus.

- ☑ Point 2 – The food really isn't that bad. I'll bring up a point that although people peg Taco Bell as a producer of poor quality meals, some of their items, like the Grilled Stuft Burrito and the Mexican Pizza, are actually pretty good. Maybe find some sort of consumer report on how a lot of people really like the taste of the food.

- ☑ Point 3 – It's a fun late night place to hang out at. I might bring in my own college experience and say that my friends and I hang out there since it stays open until 2 a.m. Make the argument that it's more than just a place to get food – it's a hang-out spot.

- ☑ Point 4 – The variety of the menu allows for mixing and matching. Say that since everything is rather small and cheap, you can get three or four items for a decent price and essentially create your own "combo meal."

- ☑ Conclusion – Taco Bell is the essence of American fast food. It's more than food, it's more than just another fast food spot - it's a classic example of a great American business that works. It brought Mexican food to mainstream America.

I'm exaggerating there on the conclusion obviously, but hopefully you get the point. You can essentially write your entire paper like this ahead of time. This way, you can use your outline to plan the whole thing and look at the big picture before you get caught up in trying to figure out how you're going to word your paper.

The worst thing you can do is start writing your paper blindly, because you'll end up rambling on about random stuff. Remember, the purpose isn't to write for no reason, or to write aimlessly. That's just like shooting in the dark. Write with a purpose, and make sure that every word you write is in that paper for a reason.

Keep asking yourself this question while you're writing:

"Will these next few sentences actually serve a purpose for me and help me to get my point across further?"

If you haven't already established the point that you're trying to make before you start typing, you've already lost.

Also remember to be careful with plagiarism. Almost all professors will run your paper through a system like TurnItIn.com, which scours the net to see if your words in the paper match anything online.

As an added protective measure to make sure you don't get nailed for plagiarism when you don't deserve it, consider saving every draft of your paper separately as you're writing it. If you do three drafts, and you save all three drafts, you can show the professor the natural progression of your work in case of a fluke mix-up, and this should leave you in the clear.

How Do You Know if You're Writing in Correct, Proper English?

The first road block most students encounter comes when they worry about how to write properly. This is where Ingredient #3, "Use Your 'Grandma Voice,'" comes into play.

I'm not here to teach you the ins and outs of the English language. I'm here to make things as easy as possible on you. Your best check of whether or not your writing is correct can be done by asking yourself these questions:

"Does this sound right?"

"Does this sound like something a reasonably intelligent person would say?"

Just keep it simple.

A lot of students will crash and burn if they try to make it sound fancy, or write like Charles Dickens. That's not being yourself. That's not your lane. Make it easy on yourself, and write in your "Grandma Voice" when you're creating a paper.

"What do you mean by a 'Grandma Voice?'" you may ask.

I mean that you shouldn't speak the way you normally would in front of your friends. It's crucial that you make your writing sound like "you," but we don't need to hear the vulgar, informal "you" that the frat house sees on Saturday nights. Think about when you go to visit your grandparents. You clean up your language, you talk a little bit more formally, and you speak in complete sentences. Use your "Grandma Voice" for your papers.

If you're extra nervous about whether or not a sentence sounds right, then, by all means, do further research. Someone, whether it's your friend or your mom, will know what is right. Don't hesitate to ask if something sounds awkward or how to phrase a certain sentence. You can't do everything on your own every time.

If all else fails, look it up on the Internet. No, you shouldn't trust Yahoo! Answers for advice, but you can find legitimate grammar guides online. You can also type the wording of a specific phrase that you want to use into Google to see if you can find it in a published article. If someone used the same wording that you want to use in a *New York Times* article, you're good to go.

Be Ambitious

The interesting thing about most universities across the nation, especially the public ones, is that they really don't expect much out of you when it comes to your writing. That's good news, because most college kids write like pure shit. If you've ever had the misfortune of participating in those "peer review" sessions where you read some other student's paper and give them a review of it, you know this first-hand. Most of this stuff sounds like something an elementary school student strung together while watching "Spongebob Squarepants." So, like I've said before, you're already ahead of the curve here if you can put a sentence together.

Because of this, if you put some ambition into your writing and strive to present new, creative ideas, especially in your conclusion, your grade will definitely improve. This is Ingredient #4, "Add Some Flair." Of course, if you go too far, you'll look like a douche and be written off. But if you have an interesting idea, go ahead and present it.

Go All The Way

Once you have an interesting idea, follow through with it. Expound upon it. Keep talking about it. That's what the rough draft is for…the real rough draft – not the "let's go through the motions" assignment the professor makes you complete. Get these ideas out onto paper and explain them fully. Remember, the professor, or anyone else reading this paper, has no idea where you're going with this stuff, and they don't know what you mean in your head. You have to spell it out for them, step by step, in the paper.

Once you've got your ambitious conclusions or ideas out on paper, then you can worry about going back to tweak it and make it pretty. Keep asking yourself these questions when you're reassessing your writing:

"Would this make sense to someone who came in cold and didn't know what I was talking about?"

"What can I do to make this clearer?"

Any time you're worried "if they'll get it or not," then it's time to explain exactly what you were trying to say in the paper. Don't be afraid that you're including too much information. If it doesn't work, you can always cut it out in the end.

The Editing Process

Now that you're almost done, it's time to make things pretty by adding Ingredient #5, "Refine Your Wording."

It's best to write the paper like I just described first, where you "go all the way." After you're done, get up and do something else for a few hours. You need to take an extended break away from the paper so you can get some perspective. When you come back, you might notice error-filled sentences that looked fine when you were in the throes of writing four hours ago. It happens all the time, so it's crucial to remember to take some time away from your creation.

On the second pass, read through the paper and fix any obvious errors you run into. But, mainly focus on the overall content of the paper.

"Does this sentence help things?"

"Am I really conveying what I want to say here?"

These are crucial questions that you need to ask yourself. By the end of the second pass, or "second draft," you should have the content of the paper down.

Now, on the third pass, which you can call the "final draft," focus on making it pretty. Clean it up, add some clever ways to deliver your words, and make sure the tone of your writing flows the way you want it to. Now is the time to go for perfection. Look up a couple of fancy words you could use to score some bonus points. Make sure the paper fulfills all of the requirements the professor gave you. After you're done, print it, and then forget about it for a day or two.

Then, you'll want to revisit the paper the day before it's due. Read it over in printed form. I'll bet, with more perspective, you'll find a couple more errors, and you'll come up with new ways to explain certain points you've made. Run through it one more time and tweak it to your liking.

The truth is, you could do this for the rest of your life and still find more work to do. No paper will ever be perfect. But, if you put this much effort into quality control and making sure that your paper is written the right way, I guarantee you will see an improvement in your grade next time. Congratulations on getting the damn thing done.

An Extra Note on Research Papers

We're going to refer to a "research paper" as an assignment that doesn't include your own opinion and requires scholarly research sources. For whatever reason, the professors that assign these types of papers prefer the tone to be more professional and dry than their contemplative essay counterparts. You also won't be asked to give an opinion in most instances. Research reports are all about being non-biased and objective. That's okay. It's just time to switch the writing style up a little bit.

For ideas on how to get your tone right, head over to CNN.com or Time.com and check out the news section. Instead of writing in a contemplative tone like you would if you were writing a paper on a novel, you need to switch it up to stern-faced, news reporter mode this time. Read a few articles and notice how the tone changes. There are no contractions in the writing, there is no wit, and the story does not really flow. In fact, it is kind of a chore to read, and it is boring as hell. That's all part of the formal style. While your research paper might be a lot more boring and dry to write, that's the way you've got to do it. Play by the rules, keep your opinions to yourself, and you'll be fine.

CHAPTER 6

How to Write a Paper on a Book You Haven't Read

I pulled this trick off numerous times during my college career. This is an extra gift to all you slackers out there.

Here's the scenario. You're assigned some bullshit book for class, and you have no intention of reading it. Unfortunately, after the class is done reading the book, you're expected to write a paper on it - a paper that you're also not interested in writing.

Well, here's what you can do. For one, show up to class for the last couple of meetings when the book is going to be discussed. Write down the conclusions that the professor emphasizes when he or she is leading the class discussion. Write down what the blowhard students who volunteer to talk are saying too. You want to collect as much information as you can on what the "hot topics" are going to be for the paper so you make sure you've got Ingredient #1 and Ingredient #2 covered.

Next, if you can find SparkNotes, PinkMonkey, or CliffNotes, get them and read them. Again, you want to get as much information on this book as possible. You can even read reviews of the book on Amazon.com to get plot point information and interpretations of the book.

To cover Ingredient #4, if you want to use a conclusion you found online, just make sure to change the words. Think of it as writing your own explanation for someone else's conclusion. You can start by thinking of synonyms that you can swap out for the key words. After that, swap out the original phrasing for your own by restructuring the sentences.

For example, let's say the conclusion you wanted to incorporate into your paper is:

"I really thought that Michael's character represents the struggle for power in the typical American male, and the baggage and bad decisions that come inevitably with that territory."

You want to paraphrase this, and make it sound like your own. So you could write something like this:

"I've come to the conclusion that the character of Michael is a metaphor of sorts for greed and power in today's economy. While he endures major struggles throughout his life as a result of his reckless actions, his tale is a cautionary one for hot-headed contemporary males everywhere."

Notice how I used different words that were similar enough to keep the point the same. Also, you need to switch up the structure of the sentence a bit. Instead of saying "Michael's character," I said "The character of Michael."

Be careful though. You always need to err on the side of caution here. You can borrow the ideas, but it needs to be unrecognizable from the original for you to avoid getting flagged for plagiarism. If you're not sure it's okay, don't include it.

At this point, you should understand the plot of the book and the point that you need to make with the paper. You can now write the paper on the book, because you understand the story. Your only obstacle now is that you'll have to include multiple quotes from the book that support your argument within the paper.

Write your paper using your "Grandma Voice" (Ingredient #3,) and make all the points you want to make. Don't include any quotes yet. Just write the whole thing, make your conclusion based on the plot or the interpretations you've heard about or read about online, and finish it.

Now, here's where the magic starts. Look for points within the paper where you can include generic quotes. For instance, if you wanted to bring up the setting's impact on the narrative of the book, now would be a perfect opportunity to insert a quote like, "The beautiful sunset covered the farmland like a warm blanket." Where do you find this quote? Just start thumbing through the book and look at random sentences. You don't need to spend more than a couple of minutes doing this.

After you've found something you want to use, read a couple of the surrounding pages just to make sure that the quote is what you're saying it is. With that setting example above, if the sunset description were during a dream sequence, you would be screwed. Spend an extra minute double-checking that you can use the quote.

If you can, throw in one quote that actually means something and isn't just a generic one. If you're completely clueless on where to start, you'll probably be able to find famous quotes online. Find the famous quote, but then look to quote something similar to it that occurs in the paragraph before. This will make it look like you choose the non-obvious quote and that the book "meant something" to you.

The bottom line is, you'll be graded on the entire paper, and not on your quotes. So, as long as the quotes you put in can serve as a voucher that says, "Yes, I did read this book," then you're in the clear. It sure beats the hell out of wasting God-knows-how-many hours reading a book you could care less about.

CHAPTER 7

Bullshitting Homework Assignments

Who the fuck does homework in college? Even though homework seems like a high school thing, you might get stuck with a douchey professor who will make you do garbage little assignments at home during your college years. Hopefully, you did the homework that counted and picked a professor who doesn't give out homework assignments in the first place (see Chapter 2.) But if you're still stuck with shit to do, here's how to get through it the easy way.

Trial and Error With Direction

Does anyone ever get less than half credit on something like a math homework assignment? You can turn in total garbage, and it doesn't even matter. Most of the time you'll get at least half credit for turning in anything at all. But, before you start putting total trash on paper and turning it in expecting full credit, you need to find out how harshly these assignments are going to be graded. You're going to have to do this the old-fashioned way – through trial and error.

Math Assignments

If you're doing a math assignment, for the first assignment of the semester or quarter, actually do the work. Let's say there are ten questions that you have to do. Do eight of them correctly. But here's where it gets fun.

Next, pick a random question, do the work correctly, but then put the wrong answer on purpose.

Then, take another question and completely bullshit it. Don't even try to come up with the right answer. While "showing your work," put down calculations that look reasonable, but are wrong. It should look obviously wrong and suspect to anyone if he stopped to read it.

To keep this experiment clean, don't put the two incorrect answers back to back, or as the first or last questions. Pick questions three and seven, for instance, to insert the wrong answers for this experiment.

Now, turn the assignment in. When you get the results back, you'll know if your professor or TA is actually reading and grading your work, or if they're just giving you credit blindly for turning in a piece of paper with numbers on it. If you're super paranoid about this process, you can repeat this exercise for the second assignment to see if you can get away with it again. But, in most instances, once should be enough for you to gauge how the grading is going to be for the rest of the course. If they don't grade the assignment at all, feel free to bullshit away!

If they're actually grading your work, you're shit out of luck, and you'll have to do the work (assuming you don't copy the answers out of the back of the book, which is definitely a viable option as well.) If they give you credit for the one with the wrong answer but the right work, and no credit for the completely made-up one, then they grade on effort and not correctness. This is definitely worth knowing, and it will still save you time. If this is the case, then you can do these assignments at 2 a.m. when you're drunk and you'll still be fine. You can relax about getting the exact figures correct for your math assignments. Instead, the name of the game becomes conveying that you know what you're doing in general.

Short Answer Assignments

You already know how to write full papers like a pro now. A short answer assignment is no big deal. The assignment will be formatted typically like a five-question print-out quiz on a book you were supposed to read, for example.

We're going to use the same approach as we just did with the math assignment. Let's say there are five questions. Answer three correctly. Then, pick a random question and answer it correctly, but answer it like a third grader would answer it. Use poor grammar, make it a run-on sentence, and make it sound like you were drunk when you wrote it. For the last question, just put mindless garbage that has nothing to do with the assignment or the book at all.

No, you don't want to be blatant and write, "I partook in a *Fast and the Furious* marathon last night and did shots of cheap vodka any time a corny line of dialogue came up" as your answer. Throw in words that look like they belong in the context of the assignment, but make it so that anyone actually reading the assignment would be like, "What the hell is this person talking about?"

Turn it in, and see what happens. Keep in mind, if they give you full credit for the answer you wrote like a child, but no credit for the pure bullshit one, then you'll know they're reading for content, but they're not grading on writing style at all.

In any event, homework sucks. But if you can find a way to save time by using techniques like these, you might find homework becoming a new amusing hobby of sorts.

CHAPTER 8

Dealing With Group Assignments

How much do you hate group projects? Before you can say, "This isn't fair," your professor will stick you with three or four randomly selected students (who are probably dumbasses, douchebags, blowhards, or a combination thereof) and part of your precious grade will be determined by some bastard child of an assignment that the four of you miraculously piece together after countless hours of pure hell. In my opinion, the group project is the worst part of the college experience, hands down. I'll tell you why.

In every other facet of college, at least everything is on you. You have independence. If you only need to study for the test for an hour, then that's it. If you can knock out a paper on a book you haven't read in 30 minutes, then more power to you. The group assignment forces you to work with other people, and by working with other people, you'll inevitably have to waste your time and do things you don't want to do. You're playing, at least partially, by the rules of your classmates now.

How many times have you been in a group setting and this happens?

"Well, guys, let's just meet on Friday at 7:00 to get some work done."

Reluctantly, you cancel your date for the night and join The Joy Luck Club during prime drinking hours at the library.

After three hours of mindless meandering, you end up with a half page of notes on nothing, and another appointment to meet next Tuesday and do the same shit.

This, in fact, can go on for weeks, until there's only a few days left before the assignment is due. At that point, someone in the group finally steps up, kicks it into gear, and gets the entire thing done in a couple of hours.

Has this happened to you? I'm sure it has. The problem here is that, just like any other social situation, lines need to be drawn and established from the jump. Within the first couple days of working together, everyone in the group will size each other up, and everyone's role will be determined. Here's a quick rundown of the typical group members you'll run into at least once during your college career.

Terrible People to Have in a Group

The Bossy Bitch/Asshole Who Doesn't Know What They're Talking About – This is the worst type of person to have in your group. They'll insist on multiple group meetings per week, even though no work is getting done, and make it seem like you're not pulling your fair share of the work just because you don't show up all the time. They'll also pull the "I'll tell the professor that you aren't helping out enough" card on the drop of a dime, for no warranted reason.

The Blowhard – A close cousin to the "Bossy Bitch/Asshole Who Doesn't Know What They're Talking About," this character is typically female, and is just as annoying as her relative. However, she's more of an approval-seeker, and she's typically a little smarter. She'll play strictly by the rules, and her goal, above all else, is to not get anyone pissed off at her.

The Stoner Who Doesn't Give a Fuck – This guy just plain won't show up to meetings, do any work, or bother to pull any weight. He might end up dropping the class without communicating it to the group, or he might just hope he can ride everyone else's coattails and get a reasonable grade. All he wants to do is get off academic probation, hit some bud, and listen to Slightly Stoopid.

The Bad Ass Who Doesn't Give a Fuck – He'll produce the same outcome as the stoner – he won't do any work – but he'll be a dick about it. He'll say stuff like, "I'm not going to do any work. What are you going to do about it?" These guys are worthless piles of shit.

The Flaky Girl – This girl seems like she could have potential, but she turns out to be a total flop. After a couple of weeks in the group with her, you realize she's not going to contribute. While she won't return your text messages, she does it in a more polite, save-face type of way than the stoner or the bad ass. Maybe it's because she's a pretty girl that the guys in the group will cut her slack. The reality is that she's just as much of an asshole as her two male counterparts.

The Moron – This guy or gal will just be an idiot. They're nice, they show up, they go with the flow, but they just don't contribute anything worthwhile and they really just slow things down. You might wonder how these clowns even got into college.

Okay People to Have in Your Group

Regular People – They're just normal people. They don't boss people around, they get work done, they're reasonably smart, and they're on point. If you get a group full of these people without any of the personality types listed above, you're in great shape. The only downside to your average Joe or Jane is that they will definitely take orders from the bossy types, and they'll also take shit from the losers in the group. They won't think outside of the box, and they'll want to meet more than you need to. Of course, in the end, they're better than slackers.

Good People to Have in Your Group

People With a Sense of Humor – Anyone who's not taking this group project too seriously is on the right track. They know this is just one dumb assignment, and that it's going to be a pain in the ass to work together. But they also know that the group should get things done as quickly and painlessly as possible. They're laid back in attitude, but serious about getting work done.

People Who Like to Look for Shortcuts – Anyone who is looking for a way to get your project done while putting a minimal amount of effort in will probably be your best friend in the group. He or she might have even read this book too. Needless to say, these people are on your side.

Good Leaders – You'll eventually end up having one person step up to the plate and take charge. Instead of getting a person of the loser variety, if you get someone that has a good, respectable, laid-back attitude, let that person be the one in charge. It will be more work for you to be in control and get stuck managing malignant personalities. If this person can handle the job, surrender it, and be friendly toward them.

Establishing Yourself to the Group

Now that we've identified all of the potential players, let's develop a philosophy on how you should project yourself to your rag-tag group. What's your objective here? I'm sure you have this ingrained into your brain by now...

To get an 'A' while doing as little work as possible on your part.

Now, in a group project, it isn't fair to your other group members to make them do the whole thing. You don't want to be like the stoner and just flake out on everybody. Also keep in mind that most of these projects have "Group Evaluations" that you have to fill out at the end. If everyone else in the group says you're a tool, then you risk getting a crap grade or, at the very least, a meeting with the professor to explain yourself. You don't want that meeting.

Let's be real here; I'm sure you want to do your fair share of the work too. You just don't want to have these people dictating your schedule and taking up all of your time because they don't know how to do work efficiently. So the modified objective for the group project is...

To get an 'A" by making yourself seem like a team player and doing your fair share of the work, and accomplishing this as easily as possible.

That's what we're aiming for here.

For most of these group assignments, you can do the work easily at home. There can be one or two meetings in the beginning where you divvy up the work and discuss the objective of what you're trying to accomplish with the entire assignment. But you don't need to hold hands in the library to get this stuff done. You can get it done at home. If you're doing an oral presentation as part of this, then you'll also need to meet at the end to practice together. If you're writing a paper, you'll need to meet at the end to put it all together and make the paper flow. Other than that, the meetings are frivolous.

So, to counteract Andy the Asshat asking you to meet every two days for four hours, the mantra to remember here during your initial meetings is "**I'm busy**." Let's repeat that again.

You're busy...

Super busy...

You play club volleyball, hold two jobs, and an internship...

You have no free time...

Your parents are coming into town this weekend...

You have **no free time!**

Of course, you don't need to actually be busy to throw out these types of excuses. If the biggest thing you accomplished this week was watching the entire first season of *Gilmore Girls* on DVD, then more power to you. Who cares? Just lie. These people aren't your friends yet, so you can say whatever the hell you want to them, and they're not going to care or know the difference. All you need to do is keep up the appearance of being a team player, and you do that by not being noticeably flaky.

Make it clear from the beginning that it's going to be difficult for you to make the group sessions. Drop little hints without being explicit about it by saying stuff like, "Fuck, I have this crazy meeting for my internship after this and I still need to make a PowerPoint for it after class."

Just talk about what a fast-paced life you live. Obviously you shouldn't overdo it, but if you've planted the seeds correctly, when it comes time to meet and you can't make it, then it's a lot more reasonable to assume that you're actually busy instead of bullshitting.

That being said, you should still show up to the first couple of meetings. You'll actually get crucial stuff done during this time, and you'll also get to know the group. Remember, the only objective here, besides doing your fair share of the work and not feeling like an ass for your own piece of mind, is to make it **seem** like you're a team player. The more face time you put into the meetings, the more it seems like you're involved.

After the first couple of meetings, you don't need to go every time. As long as you stay in contact with the group, get your work done, and send your work to everyone else via e-mail, you'll be in good shape. Always give an excuse that is job or extra-curricular activity-related though. Don't say, "Yeah man, I'm just too hungover to show up right now," even if other people in the group give the same excuse. You never want to give anyone a reason to resent you.

You need to show up from time to time, but if you can space these appearances out evenly, by showing up at every second or third meeting, it will look like you're there more than you actually are. If the group actually does meet in reasonable intervals, you might even want to show up and participate in group camaraderie. It's all up to you.

How to Direct Productivity During the Meeting

When you do end up at a meeting, chances are people will start fucking around or go off on inefficient tangents.

"Let's have everyone come up with five good ideas for the paper, and then we'll all go around the room and share!"

"Let's all write a rough draft of our separate sections of the paper and make it due, within the group only, next Friday!"

Fuck that.

When these types of suggestions come up, you need to direct the flow of traffic back to productivity, in a polite way. If the rough draft thing comes up, for instance, say something like, "You know, when I write, I tend to get it all knocked out at once. How about we make a more serious draft due in two weeks? Then we can spend the last couple of weeks doing little tweaks and we'll already be ahead of the rest of the groups in the class."

Drop a False Time Constraint

Also remember to always have a false time constraint. If you're not familiar with that term, I lifted it from "pick-up guide" books on how to hook up with girls. The big shot playas in these books always say that when you go over to introduce yourself to a random girl at a party, you should always drop a "false time constraint." You would say something like, "Hi, my name is Dave. I can't stay for long because I'm with friends, but I wanted to come and introduce myself." It's supposed to make it seem like you have high social value because your time is valuable, and it also takes pressure off the girl so she doesn't immediately start worrying that you're going to hit on her for an hour without leaving.

Regardless of what works in the pick-up world, this will definitely work in the group project world. We don't care if the other members think we have high social value, but we want to have an established time where, whether or not this meeting is coming to an end, you're getting the hell out of there.

So, when you come in, say something quick and friendly, but work your point into the mix. You want them to know that you're going to be out of there at a certain time. Pick a timeframe that seems reasonable, and establish it from the jump.

"Hey guys. Did you watch that new episode of 'Breaking Bad' last night? I know, it was crazy! It's 1:00 right now, so I've got a full two hours to knock this meeting out. We're not going to need more time than that right? Good, because I have to be at work at 3:30."

If you handle the situation like this, the other group members can't be mad if you have to leave before the meeting is over.

What to Do When Other People Fuck Up

Let's say that you got your part of the work done, and you're two days away from turning the group paper in. You meet to put the paper together, and guess what? Natasha's part of the paper is absolute garbage. *"Can this bitch even read?"* you think to yourself. Well, you've got two options now.

Option # 1: Leave It, but Make Sure the Professor Knows Who Did What

Let's not kid ourselves here. Whoever gets counted for Natasha's part of the paper is going to get a bad grade. But that's not necessarily your problem. If the professor gives you a sheet to fill out where you explain who did what section of the project, then you're in the clear. If you have extra time, then you can help her out. But otherwise, let her go down in flames and just be focused on yourself.

Option # 2: Fix It

If this project is going to be counted as a group grade entirely, you have to do something. You can start by getting someone else from the group on your side. Remember, you need to be as politically correct as possible here.

"Hey Greg, did you think Natasha's part seemed a little off? I kind of want to fix a couple of grammatical mistakes so we don't get marked off."

Let this person agree with you, which they almost always will, and then bring it to someone else.

Once you have the majority's approval, then go in and fix it. Don't ask for Natasha's approval unless absolutely necessary. If she questions why her stuff was changed later, just say, "Oh, I was in charge of final proofreading and I just re-worded a couple of sentences to make it flow." Avoid using words like "better" and "improve," because that might insult her. You want to avoid flat-out saying that she's a shit writer. Chances are, she knows she's a terrible writer anyway, so there's no need to explain it. She'll just nod in agreement and that will be the end of it.

What to Do if You Get Stuck With All of the Work

In the early planning phases of the project, you might realize you're in a shitty position. Everyone might look to you as the smart girl or guy to lead them and dump all of the work in your lap. In an even worse case, you'll be with a bunch of apathetic assholes who won't even know where to start. If you're in a situation like this, you're going to have to step up and be the leader of this group. It's not necessarily a bad thing, because doing the majority of the work will probably be less time consuming than sitting through hours of debate-filled drivel on "what we should do during the meeting next week." At the same time, it's not fair that you have to do absolutely everything. Fuck them if they're not going to do the work.

So, what should you do? First, sift through the heap of trash you've been assigned to work with and find anyone who has a little bit of common sense. I'm sure there are at least one or two other people who have a base-level of drive and intelligence to get the job done. Come to them and say, "Hey, I'll take blah blah blah (the most difficult section of the paper,) so do you think that you can do blah blah blah (a substantially easier section?)" They'll think they're getting off easy and they'll jump at the opportunity.

If the other people aren't willing to do anything, then you can revel in excitement at the chance to screw them over at the end of the project with the group evaluation. Remember to get the other people that did any work together with you and say, "Hey, Max didn't do shit. Make sure to give him a bad peer evaluation grade." Take your anger out on them this way.

The good news is, with the group in your hands, you can dictate when everyone meets. After all that you've learned in this chapter, hopefully you keep these meetings to a minimum.

Section 3:
Studying

Now that you've tackled the assignment aspect of the college game, it's time to take on the beast of all college beasts (insert creepy girl with braces or *Lord of the Rings*-looking dude joke here.) What am I talking about? The test!

It's study time, ladies and gentleman. After finishing this section, you will have all of the skills you need to prep for the big day. Let's get started.

CHAPTER 9

Study Habits

Without a good outlook on how to approach the art of studying, you're going to be lost when it comes time to get down to business. In this chapter, we're going to address the main speed bumps that most students face when they start trying to learn material for the test.

The main thing to remember is this. You'll end up wasting time when you try to study if you don't find a way to motivate yourself to a) actually try to get the work done, and b) actually pay attention and focus on what you're doing.

Think about how many hours you've wasted during your lifetime just **thinking** about studying. You're not being productive at all when you're out getting a frozen yogurt, complaining inside your own head about how you should be at home, reading your textbook. You're also being just as useless to yourself when you're trying to read the textbook, but your mind is drifting off, thinking about the party you're going to later that night. You're not doing yourself any favors in these situations, and you're really just wasting valuable time that could be spent instead enjoying the moment.

Remember, this book is called *Cutting Corners*, and it's been written for the specific purpose of freeing up your time so you can have more fun and spend less time studying. Aside from the time you have been wasting in class, which we've already addressed, the time you waste studying is the other main aspect of your life that you can reduce significantly if you follow the advice inside these next four chapters. Let the rest of this chapter be your training so you can become someone who thinks in terms of efficiency and quality of work before anything else.

Motivate Yourself

You need to have a drive, an ambition, and a willingness to succeed if you're serious about getting your schoolwork done as easily as possible. Don't look for that motivation to be inspired by a class that you already don't care about.

"I really want to learn Gerontology!" isn't inside most of us. Gerontology is the study of old people, for those of you lucky enough to have never had a Gerontology class.

Where can you find your drive? Your drive and motivation can come simply from wanting a degree, from wanting to get studying for a test done so that you can go out and get hammered, or from looking forward to the vacation you're going to take during the summer. Maybe you just have a drive to be successful in whatever you do in life, and that's where your motivation comes from.

Don't pretend that you actually care about the material you're learning, or yell at yourself because you hate Gerontology. Wanting to learn Gerontology isn't what's going to get you off your ass to study it. But getting an "A" in the class so you can rub it in the face of your ultra-competitive friends might. Getting an "A" in the class so that you're one step closer to getting into med school might.

When you get in tune with the right motivation, it relieves a lot of the stress and anxiety associated with shitty classes. You don't have to care about something you don't care about! Let go of trying to care about Gerontology, because you won't find any motivation in that. Instead, treat Gerontology as a stepping stone to get to your goal.

Here's an example that might help you grasp this concept better. A couple of years back, I wanted to start creating funny graphics to make fun of sports players that I hated. I was going to post these graphics on my blog, but there was one problem. I knew absolutely nothing about how to work Photoshop. Even though I really could have cared less about learning Photoshop, if I wanted to get these images done, I'd have to teach myself these skills.

Do you see the difference here? If I tried to find motivation and enjoyment out of learning Photoshop, then I really wouldn't have gone anywhere with it. I just learned that stuff so I could complete my real goal of making goofy images for my blog. Even though I eventually became an expert in manipulating images in Photoshop, I still didn't "care" about any of that stuff. It's boring to me. It's a means to an end. That's all it was.

So, to reiterate the concept here, if you're in a class where you don't care about the material, don't beat yourself up over trying to like the material. The material is going to be boring, and studying it is going to suck. If you can accept the fact that you hate doing it, you won't waste energy trying to convince yourself that you like it. Simply accept that you hate it and move on. If you can look at it like, "This is my ticket to law school," or, "This is another year of partying rent free if I get an 'A' on the test and Dad is happy," then you've changed your perspective. You're working for what you want now, rather than feeling like you're studying these crappy subjects for nothing. It will make things so much easier on you.

Since this is such an important concept, I'm going to go through the whole damn thing one more time. Bear with me. It will be worth reading two more minutes of this so you can get the picture.

It's pretty difficult to willingly volunteer to do something that you don't want to do. Yet, that's exactly what we're expected to do in our society with shitty school subjects. No wonder most people hate going to class. It's against human nature, yet it's something we try to fool ourselves into doing, and then get mad at ourselves when we can't find the motivation that isn't there in the first place.

Let's say someone came up to you tomorrow and said, "Hey, tomorrow I'm hosting a festival where we plant tomatoes and listen to folk music. You should come. It starts at 5 a.m." You don't give a shit about agriculture or folk music, so there's no way in hell you would go to that.

But let's say that you actually did go. Waking up at 5 a.m. would be a drag. Throughout the course of the entire festival, you'd probably just stare blankly into the horizon, feeling miserable. That's what studying without motivation is like.

Now let's say that you were invited to this festival by a member of the opposite sex. For the guys, let's say a Victoria's Secret supermodel invited you, and for the ladies, let's say a polite, handsome gentleman, who also happens to be a billionaire, invited you.

You **still** don't give a shit about the festival. You still hate agriculture, waking up at 5 a.m., and folk music. But you're excited to go to the festival now because it's about something else. It's about you getting your freak on with a supermodel or a billionaire. And when you're at the festival, you're lively, happy, and excited, rather than grumpy, irritable, and pissed off. This is what studying for a test once you're focused on your motivation is like.

Motivation can even be something as simple as:

"Once I pass this class, I'm done with Geology, and I never have to even think about studying rocks again, for the rest of my life."

While you're studying for a test, as shitty and as boring as the material may be, you do need to find a way to zone in and get it done. A lackadaisical attitude will get you nowhere, and it's in this area where most people end up faltering. The material for these tests, in a lot of instances, isn't that hard. For subjects like Math and Accounting, it's difficult to learn the concepts, but for classes like History and Communications, it's basically just memorization. If you're getting bad grades in subjects like these, the problem isn't with your intelligence level. What you need to focus on instead is finding a way to get past your own boredom and general unwillingness to do the work, and actually start studying.

Once you've got the greater motivation in place like, "I need to get an 'A' in this class so I can join the honors program this semester," you also need to give yourself something to look forward to while studying so that the studying experience can turn into something that's at least mildly entertaining. Studying can feel instantly gratifying if you find the right stimuli that works for you.

Music

Music is the easiest way to keep you entertained while studying, and it's also beneficial in more ways than one (See "The Music Technique" later in this section.) Turn on some music while you get down to business. For the best effect, avoid aggressive, intense rap or metal music, or anything too overpowering, even if that's your favorite stuff to listen to. Also avoid anything too sappy, like love ballads or extremely slow music.

Your best bet is to find something middle of the road, with an agreeable rhythm. Think about when you go into a casual place to eat like Chipotle. The music in there isn't distracting – it just goes along with the environment and almost matches your mood. You don't want to listen to an album for the first time while you're trying to study, or have something dominate the setting and distract you.

Put on old favorites that you've heard hundreds of times before that you know the words to. You might find yourself reading your textbook and shouting out a lyric from a track like, "Whoomp, There It Is," every 15 seconds or so. This gives your mind a natural break from the bullshit that is Gerontology. It also keeps you in a somewhat lively, enjoyable mood the whole time.

You know when you go out to a party or a bar and there's fun music on in the background? It automatically puts you in that zone that makes you feel good. That's the mood that we're trying to get you in here, so that studying doesn't feel like a chore. Don't get me wrong – it is a chore, but it's a chore that's a lot more enjoyable when you're dancing around to Outkast songs while doing it.

Let the music get into the background and set the mood, but at the same time, allow your brain processing power to focus on the words you're studying. When you're having a conversation with someone and music is on in the background, you're still focused on the conversation and the words that the person is saying, even though you're listening to the music a little bit at the same time. This is exactly what we're aiming for during the studying sessions.

Turn Studying Into an Event

Here's a quick anecdote for you that will explain this next studying approach perfectly. I was having trouble finding the motivation to go to the gym, especially on cardio days. Going through the motions on an elliptical machine for 30 minutes is just about as boring as sitting through a class I don't care about. I would listen to music when I went, but it wasn't enough to keep my mind from getting bored, and those closed-captioned TVs showing Fox News sure as hell weren't going to help either.

I decided something needed to be done, and at the recommendation of my little sister, I started bringing my iPhone to the gym. I now use the Netflix streaming app on my phone, and place it on the holder in the front by the display of the machine. Now, I'm catching up on old seasons of TV shows that I've always wanted to see but never had the time to sit down and watch while I'm at the gym. It's becoming an awesome ritual for me. I actually look forward to going to the gym now because I want to see what happens next on *Sons of Anarchy*. I also never watch the show at home – only at the gym. That makes it special so I'll continue to be motivated to go to the gym.

You can take this idea and apply it to your studying. Let's say that at the end of a two-hour study session, you're going to make yourself a Mai Tai. That's your motivation for the end of the routine. **Only** have Mai Tais as a study reward – never have them when you go out – and it will become something you'll end up looking forward to.

Wanna work on your tan? Work on it while you're studying outside. You kill two birds with one stone.

Or, let's say that there's a really nice park by a lake that you really like going to but never find the time to explore. Go to that park to study, and your reward will be your time at that park.

You can even couple a new hobby with studying time. Let's say that you really wanted to learn how to shoot a gun. Make Tuesday and Thursday afternoons Studying/Shooting time, where you drive out to a Starbucks right by the gun range, study for a couple of hours, and then go shooting for an hour after. And again, don't go shooting unless you study.

The possibilities are endless, but if you turn studying into an event by pairing it with something that's fun, it will make the process easier to do and a hell of a lot more fun.

Drop the "Play Studying" Act – Shit or Get Off the Pot

If you can master your behavior with this next topic, you'll save hours of studying time and become a hell of a lot more efficient.

A lot of people feel like they're done, and that they've adequately studied, once they've read something once, or twice, or ten times. You can read this sentence a hundred times, and it's not going to do a damn thing unless you're actually paying attention. Don't waste your time "play studying."

"Play studying" is where you go through the motions of studying - reading the textbook, reading notes, etc., but your mind is somewhere else. It happens to all of us. You're studying a boring topic, and then, before you even realize it, a couple of minutes have gone by and you're deep in thought about how good the new Natalie Portman movie is going to be instead of learning material for your accounting test. You've actually moved through a page of your book (by moving your eyes back and forth on the page) without remembering a word of what you "read."

When you find yourself doing this, it's time to take a break. Of course, if you find yourself **always** doing this, then it's time to buckle up and actually focus, but if you've been going at it for 20 minutes, and then you start doing it, chances are that all you need to do is get up and clear your mind for a couple of minutes.

A lot of people will continue to try to push themselves and buckle down, but you'll find your productivity going down exponentially as time goes on during a long day of studying. Don't kid yourself, and don't fight against what you really know you should be doing. Take a break. You'll get your studying done eventually.

Taking Breaks

There's a lot of great ways to take breaks. The goal is to find something that will cause you to naturally stop thinking about the topic you're studying. In other words, you want something that will immerse you in another experience, and give your brain a break.

Taking a drive is one good recommendation. You'll start thinking about the stoplights and you'll focus on the road. You don't even have to **go** anywhere in particular. Just taking a drive for 5-10 minutes with no agenda other than to clear your mind is good enough.

Pulling out one of those intense rap or metal songs I advised you against earlier is perfect for right now too. There's nothing like jumping around to DMX's "Where Da Hood At?" to get your mind off the test.

You can also grab a glass of water. Focus on sipping it slow while taking deep breaths in between drinks. Breathe into the glass and feel the fog of your warm breath react with the ice cold water. If this starts to make you relaxed and sleepy, go with the moment, even if you end up just laying around for 20 minutes. It will pay off in the end because you'll be completely refreshed by the end of your break.

Whatever you do while taking a break – **get up.** Don't take a break from studying on your computer by going on Facebook or reading a news article online. You need to physically get up and get out of the room you're working in. This will naturally change your rhythm and allow you to recharge your batteries.

Let's Get Down to Business

Here's where we start with the nuts and bolts of studying. Don't worry – you're ready, and it's actually going to be a lot easier (and shorter) than you'd think. We're going to call the first part of the studying process where you actually learn the terms "grunt work studying." The later section, where you practice the terms and review, we'll refer to as "review time."

Before we get started, I want you to know that this book was written assuming that all of you know how to study for a test. This book isn't going to teach you any basics that are obvious, like how to read. You're all college students, and I'm assuming that you have a system in place for studying already that you're doing okay with.

The next three chapters will show you how to cut corners in your studying. You're going to build on what you already know to improve your studying skills with a variety of specialized methods. Also, I'm going to make sure you cross your t's and dot your i's and don't miss **any** steps throughout your entire studying process. You'll never have to worry about covering your bases when it comes to preparing for a test again after following this plan.

Memorized Knowledge vs. Learned Knowledge

When you're studying for a test, there's a base of testable material that you need to know. If you know all of it, then theoretically you should score 100% on the test, assuming you don't screw up during the test-taking process.

But how do you study this testable material? The short answer is – you use different techniques to study different types of material. For that reason, from here on out, we're going to separate all of the testable material into two different categories – **memorized knowledge** and **learned knowledge**.

"Memorized knowledge" consists of testable material that you'll learn temporarily and spit out onto paper the day of the test. After that, you won't really think about these terms again. Definitions, people and places, formulas, and any other type of material that only needs to be memorized for a test falls into memorized knowledge.

Here's a real world example of where you would encounter the type of material you would file into the temporary "memorized knowledge bank" of your brain. Let's say that you're looking at a menu to find a meal you'd like to order at a restaurant.

"Okay, I'll have Jimmy's Famous BBQ Burger, no onions, add pickles. I'll have the fries, cole slaw, and garlic mashed potatoes as my three side selections."

You read the menu, you temporarily memorize the order, and you tell it to your server. A month later, you probably wouldn't remember the name of the burger or what the options were for sides at that restaurant.

Now, let's say there was a special on the Discovery Channel's *Shark Week* that I read about online and decided I wanted to watch. I read that it was going to air this Thursday at 6:00 p.m. I quickly remembered that, and then went downstairs to set my DVR to record it. That's it.

If you asked me two weeks from now when that shark documentary aired, I couldn't tell you. I held onto that knowledge for the 30 seconds it took to go downstairs to set my DVR, and then my brain dumped the knowledge. I never even bothered to think about it again. It's useless knowledge to me that I don't care about. This is "memorized knowledge."

"Learned knowledge" consists of testable material that you need to comprehend to remember, and, in most cases, it eventually becomes a part of your personal knowledge base. Anything that's too long to memorize will fall into the "learned knowledge" category. Anything that you need to be able to explain the ins and outs of during a test falls into the "learned knowledge" category. Anything that you need to comprehend fully in order to master the key concepts for the class will fall into the "learned knowledge" category. These concepts will get ingrained inside of your brain after you learn them.

In your everyday life, learned knowledge topics are a part of your vast knowledge base that you carry around with you all the time. They typically tend to be topics that you're either really interested in or have a background in.

If you work at a shoe factory, even if you don't care about the amount of glue needed to put each shoe together, you probably still know that it's 2.8 oz. off the top of your head because you use that figure every day in your work. You also know the plot to *Anchorman* and can explain the entire story to your 60-year-old uncle who never saw it without batting an eyelash.

"It's about this pompous newscaster named Ron Burgundy that gets into a relationship with his co-anchor, pisses off his friends, and falls into a depression. It all ends with a weird sequence at the San Diego Zoo."

That's the difference between the two types of testable material you'll encounter during the test. Join me for this next chapter, where I teach you how to retain memorized knowledge in ways you would have never imagined.

CHAPTER 10

Memorized Knowledge

We're going to tackle memorized knowledge first because it's easier. Memorized knowledge is like the current state of Vanilla Ice's career - it's a joke.

"Why is it so easy to tackle?" you may ask.

It's easy because all you need to do is find a way to remember it temporarily until the day of the test. Then, you dump it out onto paper, leave the classroom, and forget about it for the rest of your life. It's that simple.

How are you going to remember the definition of memorized knowledge? Well, I just gave you a way to remember it in the last paragraph. If I asked you a couple days from now what memorized knowledge was, you might say that it's "a joke like Vanilla Ice's career." You may not even be able to tie that back into remembering what that was in reference to ("Oh yeah – it's laughably easy to get done, just like Vanilla Ice's career is laughably bad right now") but you'd at least remember the term.

Memorized knowledge terms are easy to remember when you bring them into your world. The more often you can tie the terms and definitions that you need to know into everyday references that you're already familiar with, the easier it will be to remember them.

Mnemonics and Anecdotes

There was a shitty 1995 movie starring Keanu Reeves called *Johnny Mnemonic*. It bombed in theaters and it was pretty terrible. But, you can thank the producers of that film, because it can serve as a reminder to you that it's hard to forget random facts when they stand out.

Why was the movie called *Johnny Mnemonic*? Well, for anyone that doesn't know, a "mnemonic" is a group of words or ideas that will help you to remember something. This movie was about a guy named Johnny (played by Keanu Reeves, in one of his worst performances ever, if that's even possible) who was able to memorize lots of information and then store it inside of his brain like his head was a hard drive. The movie is set in the future, it's really weird, and it makes no sense. The purpose of me telling you this is so that now you'll have a way to remember what the term "mnemonic" is. You can remember the movie *Johnny Mnemonic* and draw your conclusion from there. Ironically, this is how a mnemonic works.

You've probably noticed that I've used plenty of quick anecdotes already in this book, with the hope of getting you to remember the concepts outlined in this book as time goes on. Just a few pages ago, I told you about how I motivated myself to go to the gym by watching TV shows on my iPhone. I did that to help you think about how you can implement this type of behavior in your own life.

Three weeks from now, you might be having a problem finding the motivation to drive 60 miles to visit your grandmother once a week. Then you might think, "Oh yeah, that guy who wrote that book I read on college was talking about how he used TV shows to make the gym fun. That gives me a good idea. I'm going to start listening to stand-up comedy CDs on the trip to see Grandma and that could make it fun."

Now, here's how using an anecdote as a mnemonic can work with specific terms that you need to memorize for a test. Let's say that you need to memorize the difference between net income and gross income for your Accounting class. The definition is this: Net Income is the income for your company after all expenses and losses are subtracted, while Gross Income is the income for your company before you subtract expenses and losses.

"So how the hell am I going to remember the difference?" you ask.

Well, first, do you have a story from your own personal experience that you can tie to this? Maybe your mom owns her own business selling T-Shirts. Since you've been around the business your whole life, you know that her main expenses are screen printing and the cost of the blank shirts. So you can remember that her "Gross" income is the amount she makes before accounting for the costs of the shirts. "She makes a ridiculous amount of money before costs are included," you say to yourself. "In fact, she makes a disgusting amount of money! She makes a **'gross'** amount of money before costs are included." There you go.

Then, come up with another quick anecdote to remember the "net income" part. "Well, she prints shirts for the basketball team the New Jersey Nets, so I could say that the Net Income is like what she makes after the product is already made, because the printed shirt with the Nets emblem on it is the finished product."

There's a great example of something that you can memorize and then throw out of your mind five minutes after the test. But don't be surprised if you remember some of these things two or three years down the line. If the anecdote and word play are good enough, it'll probably stick around in your mind for a while, especially when you're familiar with the topic you're studying in the first place. In any event, this will at least get you through the test.

These things don't have to be perfect. In fact, they hardly ever will be. Most of the time, these anecdotes that you come up with for yourself will be something that only you will be able to understand. But that's all it needs to be. It doesn't need to be something that you have to explain to anyone else.

If you don't have a story from personal experience, then you can also just make up an extended explanation. Come up with an alternative definition to the term that only makes sense to you, that will be easy to remember. A story you'll think is funny and that you'll remember when you see the term on the test is what you're aiming for here.

Let's say that you need to remember what a sagittal crest is for your Anthropology test. The definition is this: A sagittal crest is a ridge of bone running across the top of the skull in certain animals.

"Okay," you say to yourself. "How the hell am I going to remember this one? Sagittal sounds sort of like 'sage,' which I know is a term for a wise old man. Crest is like a wave, right? So it can be a wave-shaped crest, sort of like a crown, on some wise old man's head who's like a wizard. Sagittal crest. Okay."

If the words work for you, then they work. If something doesn't flow easily and naturally, then stay away from it. If you make it too complicated, chances are you're not going to remember the mnemonic and you'll really be up shit creek. If you're relying on memorizing these anecdotes, then the whole system falls apart if you can't remember what ties everything back to the term and the real definition. Give it a chance though. Anything that you've made yourself and relates to something that's familiar to you will be inherently easier to remember than the dry definition by itself.

Analogies Your Way

You can also resort to using an analogy to remember your memorized knowledge term when you don't have a story or an extended explanation that you can make relevant for yourself.

It's effortless to remember things that you already know. I'm a huge hip-hop fan, for instance, and I know Tupac lyrics like the back of my hand. That's all memorized. No problem. So, what we're going to do is take things like, for me, hip-hop lyrics, and tie them into the terms you need to memorize for the test.

Biology may not have any relevance to your everyday life, but you can remember the term "mitosis" by recognizing it because it looks similar to the word "Mentirosa," which also happens to be the title of a classic hip-hop song by Mellow Man Ace that you know by heart. What's that song about? **Separating** from a lying girlfriend. What's mitosis? A cell **separating** into two identical sets. Boom!

That might not be a perfect analogy, but it's one I created for myself, and the more outrageous and the more of a stretch the analogy is, the easier it is to remember because it's stupid and it's funny. As long as you can remember that key word, "separate," then you'll be able to pull out the rest of the definition from your memory bank if you review well enough (we'll cover reviewing in Chapter 12.)

Here's another one. Let's say that you needed to quickly remember who the Greek philosopher Aristotle was, as well as the fact that he was one of the founders of the concept of causality. You know that the Olympics started in Greece, so you can associate him with the Olympics. And "causality" looks close enough to "casualty." You can say, "If someone got hit in the head with one of those shotput things that they throw in the Olympics, there would definitely be a casualty." And there you go.

Again, my personal favorite things to use are music references, movie references, and sports references. If your passion is baking or competitive fishing, then use references from those worlds. You need to do what works for you, and use something that you're comfortable with.

Check the Rhyme

If you really want to make it quick, you can memorize definitions for specific terms by simply rhyming them around in your head. Let's say that you have to memorize the term "ethnocentrism" for your Communications class. The definition is: the tendency to believe that your ethnic group is more important than everyone else's, and that the other group's worth is measured in relation to yours.

"Okay," you say. *"Where do we go with this one?"*

Well, my offensive mind always likes to make rude versions of words. It's one of my favorite hobbies. Football player Tim Tebow has been called "Tim Te-Blow" numerous times in my household, and Kim Kardashian has been dubbed "Kim Lard-Ass-Ian." So, let's do that with this term.

Ethnocentrism sounds like "Eth-Ho-Centrism" – and hoes think they're the center of the universe. That doesn't even need any more work. We've got that definition wrapped up right there. So when you see "ethnocentrism" on the test, say to yourself, "Oh, you mean 'Eth-Ho-Centrism?'" and use your own rhyming analogy to get the answer right.

What if you were stuck with "The Battle of Waterloo" on a History midterm? The Battle of Waterloo is Napoleon's last battle that took place in 1815. The first thing that came to my mind when trying to memorize this one was to rhyme "Waterloo" with Adam Sandler's weird saying from one of my all-time-favorite movies, *Billy Madison*, where he says, "Tay-la-la-who-whooo!" That kind of rhymes with Waterloo. I can think of the villain in that movie, Eric, as a bastard as crazy as Napoleon. If I see Waterloo written down on the test, I'll remember Sandler's annoying "Tay-la-la-who-whooo!" and remember this silly rhyming analogy I made up for myself to get the answer right.

Whether it's an anecdote, analogy, or rhyme that you're creating, you want to run through it as many times as you need until the mnemonic starts to become familiar during the grunt-studying process. You'll be drilling these things into your mind to ensure you remember them during "review time," so you don't need to worry about total memorization at this point. Just focus on creating something that you know you'll remember.

By the way, no matter how silly any of the anecdotes, analogies, or rhymes you make up are, when you're memorizing them, focus on remembering your experience creating these mnemonics instead of the logic (or lack thereof) in the actual analogy. Do any of these things actually make sense? No. But that's not the point. No matter how dumb or void of true reason your mnemonic is, if you can remember the experience of making it up, that's all you need to remember it, and thus, get your answer right.

When I have two drinks in my hand, one for myself and one that's my friend's, I'll make up a mnemonic to remember which drink is which. I'm left-handed, but if my drink is in my right hand, I'll say to myself, "Mine's on the right, because I'm not right-handed."

Does that make any sense? No.

Would it be easier to remember it if I just moved my drink to my left hand? Probably.

But I'm sure I'll recall which drink is which because what I'll remember is that I made up something odd and stupid to remember it in the first place.

Why Does This Work?

That's a good question, and I have another example that will explain it for you. Let's say you were at a party and some drunk moron felt the need to make an announcement from the second story of the house.

"Excuse me everyone. One second, please. I just want to tell you something. Did you know a giraffe can clean its own ears with its tongue?"

As soon as he said that, he slipped and tumbled down the staircase, crashing right into some geek who had no business being at the party. He knocked over the geek's drink, which splashed vodka into the geek's eye. Then, that nerd ran outside and jumped into the pool to stop the burning in his eyes. That's a ridiculous memory you would remember for the rest of your life. It's crazy, it's random, and it's funny.

Flash forward to three years later. You're at the zoo with your girlfriend and see the giraffes. What's the first thing that pops into your head? Of course, it's that dumbass yelling that giraffes can clean their ears with their tongues, and then falling down the stairs. But, the side effect of this whole experience is that you've now memorized a useless fact. You tell your girlfriend, "Hey, did you know that giraffes can clean their ears with their tongue?" and she thinks you're some sort of scholar. Swag.

Why does this happen? Why do random facts like that stick with us, almost like our "learned knowledge base" does, while the stuff that we want to memorize for tests, but find boring, falls flat?

Here's the answer. Unless you tie the new random facts you're learning onto something that's interesting or compelling to you, there's no other reason to remember it inside your brain other than "because you have to." And, like we were talking about in the last chapter, the fact that you "have to" alone won't give you motivation, consciously or subconsciously, to get the ball rolling internally.

CHAPTER 11

Learned Knowledge

Now you're going to learn how to learn learned knowledge. Was that sentence complicated enough for you? When you sit down to actually learn a new concept or term, chances are you're making it too difficult on yourself. I didn't need to make the first sentence in this paragraph so complicated. I could have said, "Let's talk about learned knowledge now." But, when I write, I like to come up with a really clever first sentence that will grab the reader's attention. Sometimes, I get too caught up in what I'm doing because I'm overthinking it, and the result is an awkward mess like that first sentence above, or this entire paragraph if you want to get technical about it. Are you making too big of a deal out of concepts you're trying to master for tests? Let's see.

We're going to start with our learned knowledge example about *Anchorman* from earlier. It's a pretty simple story about a newscaster from San Diego, right? The funny thing is that if I asked you to "study" an ancient work from 1359 called *Anchorman* and told you that I was going to give you a test on it next week, you would probably find a way to screw it up.

Since you're not interested in ancient works and you're approaching it as "studying" rather than just watching a movie and enjoying it, you'll think about it in fragments and try to look for what I, as your fictional professor, wanted you to get out of the story. You would also think in terms of what I could potentially test you on. You'll try to memorize major plot points of the story instead of just enjoying the movie.

If you're being tested on a book, or if you're being tested on a general concept like "economies of scale," it's best for you to ingrain these subjects into your internal "learned knowledge base" rather than try to memorize them. Once you actually open your mind up to these topics and learn them, there's nothing you need to worry about memorizing anyway.

For example, let's say that you read a fun article in a magazine today about beer in America. In the article, you found out that the craft brew market is growing in size, but that right now, the advertising budget of an entire craft brewery for a year is about the same as the amount spent by a major corporation like Budweiser during one primetime ad on TV. That's pretty interesting stuff to you.

When you're out drinking with your friends over the weekend and the subject comes up, you recite this information back and inform your buddies about what's going on with the beer industry. What you didn't realize is that when you read that article earlier in the week, you added all of those concepts into your "learned knowledge base," and you'll carry that around with you for years to come. You did it without trying to memorize anything.

Learning something the real way, as long as you can find a way to make it less boring, complicated, or painful, is literally just like watching a movie or reading a fun article. Did you need to memorize the movie *Anchorman*? Of course not. You might not remember every single detail of the film, but I bet if I gave you a test on it, you'd do pretty well, even if you haven't seen it in years.

Remember, anything that's too long to memorize will fall into the learned knowledge category. Anything that you need to be able to explain the ins and outs of during a test falls into the learned knowledge category. Anything you need to comprehend fully in order to master the key concepts for the class will fall into the learned knowledge category.

When a piece of testable material falls into the learned knowledge category, instead of trying to memorize it, all we're going to do is learn it with no tricks involved. Of course, if there's a learned knowledge-type concept that you don't feel like putting in the effort to learn, you can treat it like a memorized knowledge topic, and we'll cover how to do that in just a few pages. But, for maximum success, you should approach all of your learned knowledge topics by doing it the long way and just learning it straight up.

At the same time, this isn't to say that you can't review and memorize details, especially key words about the topic or major concepts that you've seen repeated by the professor and the textbook, so that you can be even more prepared. You can use your memorization techniques to assure that everything is remembered, and that extra work will act as a supplement to your newfound knowledge on all of these topics.

How Do I Learn Something?

So, how do you do it? How do you learn new things? Like everything else, it's easy and it becomes pretty routine when you can find a way to do it that works for you.

The objective when learning a topic is simple. **You need to find the correct definition or the answer to whatever this topic or concept might be, and then get it ingrained into your brain so you know it like the back of your hand.**

You can pull this off in most instances just by reading your textbook or notes, digesting what you read, and then reading it over a couple more times until it feels like you get it completely.

I know this is basic stuff here, but I want to spell everything out so you don't try to grasp at straws and strive for too much. If you sit around and think about "how" to learn something for too long, you'll waste too much time and you'll make no progress. You learn things by learning them. There's no superstar quality you need to develop to become successful at this.

The Solo Conversation Technique

Let's say that you need to learn a general concept about Art History for your test next week, and memorizing the term isn't enough. This is something you really need a grasp on. A good measure of whether you comprehend the material enough for it to become a part of your "learned knowledge base" is if it's something you're able to recite back to a friend and have a genuine conversation about while feeling comfortable. But, while you're studying, I'm sure you'd rather be alone, and I'm sure your friend has better things to do than hear you babbling on about some bullshit they don't care about. So, let's turn telling a story into a solo technique.

Once you're ready, read over your material. When you're done with it, read it again, but this time, read it out loud to yourself. When you're reading it out loud to yourself, read it one sentence at a time, and pause briefly after each sentence. Pretend that you're reading this to explain to a friend what this concept means. At the same time, in your mind while you're doing this, also do a mental check with yourself.

Ask yourself in your mind:

"Do I really know what this means?"

Keep going through the definition for this topic, sentence by sentence, until you're done with the concept and you actually feel like you have a good grasp of the topic.

The visualization of teaching the concept to your friend will cause you to feel more confident on the topic, because it's almost like you're teaching the concept to her for real. When you're able to teach someone something, you know deep inside that you're really becoming a master at it. Pretending to teach your friend, and coupling that with your own question of, "Do I really know what this means?" will cover all of your bases internally.

Now, on to the final test. Stand in front of a mirror and pretend that someone asked you to define the concept. Without looking at the book or whatever your source material is, explain what the concept is out loud. Yes, I know you look like an idiot doing this stuff, but let's just hope no one is lurking in the corners with a video camera. Define it clearly and completely.

You might not get it on the first try. You might need to do it three or four times to get it right. But you're going to do it until it flows naturally and you actually know within yourself that you've got this. There will be a point where, all bullshit aside about just wanting to be done with this and hoping that you know the material enough, that you actually **know** within yourself that you "get" this concept. That's what we're aiming for here. Get to that point, and then walk away. Don't worry, you'll be reviewing this stuff later. But once the victory occurs, move on to the next one and worry about retaining information later.

Should I Try to Learn It, or Should I Memorize It?

One quality that separates the men from the boys, or the women from the girls, is tenacity. If you follow through on everything that you do and you don't give up on finding the answers you need so that you can truly comprehend these learned knowledge topics, then you'll see your grades go up significantly. It's really that simple.

Finding a good definition or explanation for the concept you're trying to study is all you need to be focused on at first. If you don't understand the term the way it has been explained in your textbook, notes, or whatever it is you're studying, then you need to look elsewhere. Even though, technically, it is explained in your textbook, you don't have the answer yet, because **you** don't get it. Looking at an explanation that makes no sense and expecting it to work isn't enough. But, just because you don't have the answer yet, it might not be time to give up.

90% of people will start play studying if they run into this type of issue. They'll throw their hands up in the air and say, "Oh well. I just don't get this one. I've done everything I can, but it's just not working out. Too bad."

Instead of accepting defeat here, remember that that's not the only option. You can take the easy way out, which is, in some instances, the smartest thing to do. Let's cover how to do that first. This involves throwing the concept out of the "learned knowledge" category and over to the "memorized knowledge" category. Use your memorization techniques to remember the wording of the definition and key phrases, even though you don't really comprehend the concept of what you're memorizing. This will work to a degree, and you'll end up getting the answer right on the test if those specific words you memorized show up as answer choices.

For instance, if you decided to give up on learning about the background of Samba for your World Music test, then you would just remember, using your memorized knowledge techniques, that Samba is a rhythm-based type of music and that it's Brazilian.

Maybe your friend Sam is Brazilian, so you use that anecdote ("Sam is Samba") to remember the country of origin. Then you say, "Well, if I say, 'samba-samba-samba-samba' to myself in a Latin accent, it has a good rhythm to it, so I'll remember that it's rhythm-based by doing that."

Then, when you're taking the test, if there's a multiple choice question on Samba, you'll at least remember that it was something Brazilian and that it's rhythm-based, and you can use the power of deduction to eliminate other choices that could be wrong. But if there's a big short-answer question on the test like, "Explain what Samba means to the people of Brazil," then you would be screwed.

You should always strive to learn as much as you can for a test, but sometimes other factors come into play, such as limited time or a limited amount of material available to learn from. If it's not an important term that could be a major part of the test, I would recommend throwing it into the memorized knowledge category if it seems like it's more trouble than it's worth. But if you're going to take the easy way out, then take the easy way out. Don't waste time fucking around. Spend the two minutes you need on it and be done with it.

Of course, there is another option if you run into a problem finding answers. You can also go the extra mile and seek outside resources to learn the material. I would only recommend spending the extra time to do this when you have that gut feeling that it's something that you really need to learn for the test. If it's something that could potentially only earn you one extra point, then don't waste your time. Always keep in mind that your objective is to do well while putting in as little effort as possible.

Remember, when you're going to learn something to this degree, it means that you need to understand it to the point where you can have a conversation on the topic while feeling confident about it. This is when you truly "comprehend" the material. The further you are toward that point, the better off you are for the test. Again, you don't need to have this type of grasp on memorized knowledge. That doesn't require the same type of brainpower.

Actually DO IT

Let's say you've decided to move forward and seek outside resources to learn the material. Since you got nowhere with the textbook and your notes, you need to do some research. Even if you put the effort in to find the material that will help you understand the concept, you'll still run into instances where you still have no luck finding anything.

Here, most people stop. To them, since they put in that 30 minutes of effort, but still have no answer, they consider that "studying." They rationalize to themselves that they've spent enough time on that particular topic. Unfortunately, you and I both know that isn't good enough.

You should be applauded for your effort. And it sucks majorly that you've spent a half hour reading a bunch of crap and searching for answers when, in the end, you're no better off than you were at the beginning. Give yourself a hand for that. Someone needs to acknowledge that. But, as the Brandy song goes, "Almost doesn't count." It really doesn't. So as fucked up as it is that you spent the time trying, you aren't **done** until you actually know the material. You can't check this topic off your to-do list until you **comprehend it**.

A lot of our "quitting" mentality has to do with our perception of what the "normal" amount of time or effort should be to achieve something.

You might be thinking inside your head:

"Well, no one is going to study the economics term 'Economies of Scale' for more than 20 minutes, so that's all I'll study it for too."

Who said that's how long everyone else is studying it for?

And who said that these people are going to get an "A" on the test?

If it's something that you really need to know, then you shouldn't give up so easily. Don't just throw your hands up in the air and say, "I'm done" when you're not done. If you're not going to do it, don't do it. But if you know you'll get screwed if you don't do it, buckle up and actually try. Don't give up until you get it right.

Share With Friends

After you get a good grasp on your learned knowledge topics for the test, it's time to take this show on the road. You'll learn about schedules for studying in the next chapter, but, until then, keep in mind that you'll be learning this stuff over a period of at least a couple of days. Since you want to give your mind some time to rest, you need to go out and do other things once you've gotten a firm handle on your new learned knowledge.

However, while you're at the gym, getting drunk, or going out to the mall in the interim, it would serve you well to recite some of this new learned knowledge to your friends. Don't make a production out of it. But, when you remember, just share one or two of the concepts that you learned with your friend briefly. We don't want them to get bored here (that's why you're doing "The Solo Conversation Technique,") but reciting a couple of these concepts out loud to real live people will allow you to re-confirm with yourself that you understand these topics. Just make sure to keep things brief. We don't want your friend running away from you because he can't bear to hear any more about Gerontology.

CHAPTER 12

Review Time

Congratulations! You're done with the "grunt work studying." Now, it's time to lay out all of the work you've done in one place so you can start "review time." You don't want to have to keep referencing a book or a bunch of scattered pages of notes when you're ready to review. You want it all in one spot.

We're going to refer to the study guide that you make as your "review sheet" for the rest of the book. Now, let's walk through how to make a review sheet efficiently and for maximum effect.

The Re-Writing Technique

You might want to make your review sheet as you go when you first start studying, so that your notes will be fresh. Again, let's split things up in terms of memorized knowledge and learned knowledge.

Let's start with memorized knowledge. First, write out the term. Then, right next to it, write your mnemonic device. Whether it was a rhyme, an anecdote, or a completely irrational analogy, put down whatever is going to help you to remember the term. Next to that, write the actual definition, accurate to the wording of the professor or the book. You want to be sure that you include every key word that you need to know. All of this stuff needs to be right there. Under that, you can even write the definition in your own words if that helps.

Here's an example of what you want the review sheet to look like:

Ethnocentrism - Eth-Ho-Centrisim - "Hoes" Think They're The Center Of The Universe - The tendency to believe that your ethnic group is more important that everyone else's, and that the other group's worth is measured in relation to yours.

In other words, since I'm Italian, I would think that Italian people are more important than everyone else, and that we're better than everyone else.

You can quiz yourself on the material just like you would with flash cards. Cover up the side with the definition and your mnemonic device so you can only see the term. Then, try to produce both the mnemonic device and the definition in your head or out loud. It's that simple.

"Can I type this instead of hand-writing it?" you may ask.

You can, but you'll miss out on the full effect. If you physically go through the process of hand-writing this stuff, it requires you to process the information while you're putting it onto paper more than it would if you had just typed it. We're all so efficient in our generation at typing that we do it without thinking about it, and if you actually write something down, it takes that extra step to think about it, which works a lot better for what we're trying to do here.

Remember, all of this memorization stuff is a matter of repetition. By re-writing everything down on a piece of paper again, it gives you another hardcore drilling of the information, and you get more familiar with it.

On top of that, you'll also become more confident with the terms that you're learning. When you're writing down the definition of "sagittal crest," and, as you're writing it, you realize, "Hey, I know this and I don't even need to look at the textbook to find the definition," you'll start to realize that your brain is really starting to gel with this stuff.

After you're done with the memorized knowledge, it's on to the learned knowledge.

Follow the same format – take a piece of paper, write the term or concept down, and then write down everything that you need to know. But try doing this without any references to the textbook or your source material. After you're done, look back at the source material and make sure that you got it right, and that everything that you need to know is completely there, in the right form.

It's a good exercise to write the stuff out without reference to your source material, because it serves almost as a pre-test. You'll verify to yourself that you really comprehend the material. But remember, you're going to use this review sheet as your only real source of reference from here on out. If you put something wrong on here, you're going to be drilling garbage into your brain instead of the real answers, so make sure to check your work and keep it error-free.

You may also wonder how long your review sheet should be. The easy answer is, as long as it needs to be. For a longer and more thorough test, the sheet could easily be five pages, front and back. For an easier test that you're pretty confident with and doesn't contain that many major topics, it could be a single sheet.

Don't let the length limit you. Do you think Francis Ford Coppola gave a fuck that *The Godfather* was three hours long? Hell no. Sure, most movies are two hours, but the plot and the epic nature of his movie required three hours. So, he made it three hours long. But at the same time, do you remember any bullshit sequences in *The Godfather* that didn't need to be there? No. It was jam-packed with quality scenes, and every minute was relevant to the story.

With your review sheet, which isn't going to be as riveting as *The Godfather*, you don't need to worry about the length, but you also don't want to make it excessively long. Don't fill it with every single detail that's not relevant. Remember, you can always go back to the book if you really need to. If you create a review sheet that's too detailed, you're going to lose yourself in it while you're reviewing and you won't be able to study efficiently. So, finding a healthy balance is the key.

Review Mechanics

Now that you have your review sheet laid out and ready to rock, the hard work is over. You've finished all of the groundwork for your studying, and by this point, you should feel pretty confident about your chances going into the test. Congratulations.

All that's left now is to review the material multiple times, so the terms become more ingrained into your brain. Once they become very familiar, either in a memorized way or in a learned knowledge way, you can consider yourself **done**.

So, how do you review effectively? First of all, once you've finished the review sheet, feel free to run through everything once to make sure it's all correct. After that, take a long break of at least three hours, but preferably overnight, before you even look at this stuff again. You need the time off so you don't burn yourself out.

When reviewing, approach it like everything else we've done in this book so far. **Make it easy on yourself.** This isn't the time to play "imaginary drill sergeant" on yourself. Once it feels like you know it, then it's time to stop.

As you can tell by now, I'm a big fan of using mnemonic, audio, and visual devices to remember testable material. Here are a couple more techniques that you can add to your arsenal of study weapons that will help during review time.

The Music Technique

While music is awesome to use during the initial grunt-work stages of studying because it helps you to stay entertained, during the review stages it can become even more useful. Do you ever drive down a street and end up remembering the song you were listening to in your car the last time you were there? Music has a powerful effect on our memory, just like our sense of smell does. Do you ever smell cookies baking and then remember your Mom waiting for you after school with a fresh batch of Snickerdoodles? Crazy, huh?

Even though the routine of reviewing for these tests can get pretty ho-hum and indiscernible, you might be able to squeeze a couple of extra answers out of your mind come test time that you wouldn't have gotten otherwise by employing a strategy I call "The Music Technique."

When you're reviewing, all you have to do is listen to music. While you're in your mind focusing and re-reading one of the terms, the song that's on at the time will be, consciously or not, paired with this experience of reading that specific term. And yeah, if you review this stuff eight times, you might have eight different songs that got paired with each term. It doesn't matter.

Here's what does matter. When you're taking the test, and you see a term that looks familiar, but you're drawing a blank on it, you might not remember the definition, but you will remember the experience of studying it. You might remember specific words that you wrote down on the review sheet, and you might remember that you were listening to The Black Keys when you studied it. That memory of that song gives you another pathway back into your brain. It will give you an opportunity to think about the experience you had reviewing the term.

Then, you might get lucky and remember the term, or at least remember more about the definition of the term, which will help you pick out the right answer if you're in a multiple choice scenario. You'd be surprised how well this strategy works. You really have to try it for yourself to get the full understanding of it. Again, it isn't what you want to rely on, but consider it a last-resort backup if all else fails.

The Visual Technique

In the same vein as "The Music Technique" is "The Visual Technique." When reviewing, take about a minute during each review session to study the way that your review sheet looks. Don't read the words, don't look too closely, but look at the piece of paper, with your chicken-scratch handwriting and all, and study it, almost like it were a piece of art. Look at the way a certain term happened to be more indented on the line than the next one, or how the definition on one line ended up going only half way across the line and left a blank spot on the paper. Don't get too weird with it, but definitely give your whole review sheet a full glance-over like that.

While taking the test, if you get stuck on a term, stop for a second and try to remember your review sheet. Do you think you can remember what the paper looked like? Maybe you might remember that this term, even though you forgot what it was called, was two-thirds of the way down on the review sheet and it started with an "O." I'm not saying you're going to pull in some genius photographic-memory powers here, but this technique can at least help you replay your situation of studying. It's another tool you can use to recall your studying experience during the test.

Creating a Schedule

Now that we've gotten **how** to study down, let's talk about **when** you should study. Let's look at your objective here. **You want to get an "A" in this class with the least amount of effort possible.** So, in this sub-section, I'll show you how to plan your studying schedule according to your specific circumstances.

If you've been going to class this whole time, you're really into the material, and you know ahead of time what's going to be on the test, then, by all means, start your grunt-work studying one to two weeks ahead of time, and have the review sheet done a good five to seven days before the test. Start reviewing three days before the test, two times a day, and then amp it up to three times on the day before the test. Review one more time the day of the test (we'll deal with that specifically in Section 4,) and you should be good to go.

Now, if you haven't been going to class, you'll probably need to wait until that all-important review lecture or "study guide lecture" that we talked about earlier in Section 1. There, you'll learn about most of the buzz words that will appear on the test. If this is the case, then don't even think about studying before then. There's no point. Even if the review lecture is two days before the test, it's still enough time to grind out this entire process. Your schedule would look something like this:

Day 1 – Review Lecture
Go home and get 75% of "**grunt-work studying**" done

Day 2 – Morning – Get the other 25% of "**grunt work studying**" done
Afternoon – Get the review sheet written
Evening – Review about three times

Day 3 – Morning – Review one more time
Afternoon – Test

This isn't an ideal schedule. It's worst-case. If you have more than two days, then you should spend at least an extra day letting that review sheet marinate in your mind and then do four to five review sessions the day before the test.

The more times you can review without burning yourself out, the better. But also be careful of reviewing a lot of these terms, especially the memorized ones, too far out before the test. You won't remember this stuff for that long. If you're drilling yourself with memorized knowledge a week before the test starts, you're taking it too far. Don't start the review process until three days before the test, max, for any regular college course.

If your professor doesn't provide a study guide lecture and you're also skipping class, then you're on your own time completely. Find the resources you need to get the material, whether it's from the textbook, friends who took the class in semesters past, online, or whatever. Then, get to work whenever you want to. Again, just don't start the heavy reviewing until a couple days before the test.

What if You Screw Your Schedule Up?

Like all things, schedules were made to be broken. You can have an airtight, fool-proof schedule for the day, and chances are you won't be able to completely abide by it. Things come up. Plans change. People you rely on screw you over. The bottom line is, you can't lay out every moment of your day and expect it to actually work. That's why, when scheduling out your studying, make the plan very vague, with lots of room for free time.

What if you end up getting burned out and you're "just not feelin' it" after 30 minutes, even though you scheduled out a two-hour block to study? Don't push yourself into more studying. Take a break, and then adapt your schedule later in the day to make up for that lost time. You won't know for sure how long this stuff will really take to complete, but, when done efficiently, studying can take a lot less time than you originally thought.

Section 4:
The Day of (and Night Before) the Test

At this point, you're ready for the test. Prep is over. You've got it down, and you know it. Now it's time to enter the arena and play the game.

All of that work you've put in so far means nothing if you bone it when it's actually time to take the test. You can be the best player on your basketball team during practice, but if you suck ass during the game, you'll end up riding the bench.

Even though Kobe Bryant is still the best player at the Lakers' practices, he rakes in the big bucks because he's built a reputation on being able to hit the clutch shots and deliver during important games. Not everyone can do this. Some of the most talented players around (LeBron, anyone?) end up dropping the ball when it's time to win a championship.

But don't worry, because I've got you covered. You're going to learn how to win test-taking championships (if there is such a thing) during this section. With the right skillset in place, you'll be able to see all of that hard work you've done studying pay off with a great score on the test.

CHAPTER 13

Getting Ready Before the Test

Day Before the Test Prep

Your prep before the test doesn't just include studying. What we want to do here is make everything as stress-free and drama-free as possible on your test day. If you can get in, do your business, and get out, everything's going to work out fine. If you're running down the halls to get to the test on time, or, even more stupidly, if you're waiting in line at the student store, buying your Scantron 10 minutes before the test, you're causing yourself unnecessary stress. Get all of that stuff done the day before the test, where you can do it at a leisurely pace. Hell, you can even buy Scantrons in bulk so you never have to worry about making a special trip to buy one.

Let's go through things that you might need for the test:

___ Scantrons

___ Blue Books for writing essays

___ A calculator

Here are some extra things that you need to have handy as well which I'll discuss later on in this chapter:

___ Your review sheet

___ An iPod (or whatever MP3 player you use)

___ Headphones (preferably both earbuds and noise-cancelling ones)

___ A light-reading magazine

___ Your phone

___ A protein bar

___ A drink (don't pack this ahead of time – just take a cold one out of the fridge on your way out the door)

Get all of these things ready to go and zipped up in your backpack the night before the test. This will create less stress for you in the morning, so you don't have any moments of scrambling. Now, let's talk about what **not** to do before your test.

Don't Be Stupid

What have I been hammering into you this whole time? What is your objective? **To get an "A" in the class, with a minimum amount of effort** on your part. So, if you can't perform during the hour or so that you have to take this test, everything that you've done so far means nothing. You might as well have been rolling blunts and playing *Call Of Duty* this whole time. It would have been a lot more fun, and, frankly, it would have been a better use of your time, since it was something that you would have actually enjoyed doing.

No matter what, you need to keep yourself in tip-top shape the night before and the morning of your test. **Don't go out until 3 a.m. and get trashed the night before your test.** If you're hungover, you're going to be at about 50% brain capacity for the test, and you don't want that. You want a clear head, you want to be relaxed, and you want to have calm, focused, warrior-esque composure so you can attack this motherfucker of a test and then get out of the classroom.

As soon as you're done with the test, feel free to buy a fifth of vodka and down it on your way back to your dorm room. Just give yourself a fighting chance during the test by staying sober and well-rested.

Now I know some people like to get a little buzzed or a little high before the test because it "loosens them up" or calms their nerves. You and I both know that even though you might be more relaxed when you do this, you're definitely also losing brain capacity. So, for those of you that fit into this category, I ask this of you: read the rest of this section, and give it one honest chance this way without any substances involved. If it still doesn't work for you, then at least you gave it a shot.

Last-Minute Scheduling

If you've planned it right, you shouldn't be studying past 10:00 p.m. the night before the test. This way, you can mentally detach yourself from all of the crap you've been studying, and give yourself enough time to focus on something else before you get to sleep. If you can turn on a funny movie, watch your favorite TV show, or play some video games for about an hour after the studying has been done but before you go to sleep, this will be a major benefit.

Everyone else in your class will be cramming material into their heads until 2 a.m., and they're going to be stressing themselves out by reading the same lines from the textbook over and over again without being able to focus. You, on the other hand, are going to be playing *Halo* with your buddies, or watching *New Girl*. Go for a drink or two if you want. Just make sure that it's under the amount that's going to make you feel like shit the next morning.

Also, don't try to go to sleep early the night before the test. If you're used to going to sleep at 1 a.m. and that's what you do every other night, tonight is no exception. If you try to go to sleep at 9, you're just going to lay around, restless, trying to fall asleep, and your sleep quality for the whole night will end up being worse. Go to bed at the same time, follow your routine, and make it feel natural. Do what makes sense.

When you wake up, take a deep breath. It's not a big deal that you have a test today. All it's going to be is an hour out of your day to take it, and about 20-30 minutes of review at various times before the test. That's it.

Racking Up Points

Before we even start our last-minute review, let's look at a general philosophy on how to approach taking a test. It's another one of those ideas that just makes things simple, so you don't have to run around inside your head all day trying to figure out what to focus on. It goes like this.

Each test is simply points. It's out of 100 percent. Therefore, your goal as a test-taker is to secure as many of those points as possible. Hopefully, you can get 100 out of 100 points. But maybe you'll only get 70. Who knows? In any event, the only thing you need to be thinking about is getting points.

Points are non-discriminatory. If each multiple choice test question is worth 2 points, then a bullshit question like, "What class are you in right now?" is worth the same amount as, "Which three symbolic references are most apparent in Shakespeare's *Hamlet*?" This is obviously a really simple concept, but it's worth pointing out.

Your goal is to score points, and the best way to assure that you get the maximum amount of points on the test is to make sure that you don't fuck up on the easy questions. You need to secure those points as efficiently as possible. The questions that you're not sure about, you have a lower probability of getting right anyway, so those are put on a lower priority while you're taking the test.

Keep asking yourself during the test:

"What actions can I take right now that will allow me to get the most points on the test?"

We'll go through how to approach the test so that you can get the maximum amount of points during the next chapter, but just keep this in the back of your mind until then.

Last-Minute Review Time!

On the day of the test, a main stress factor for you will be getting to campus on time. Whether it's a three-minute walk from the dorms or a twenty-minute commute, you want to give yourself plenty of time. Since you want to have a clear head while doing your final review, get over to campus and plan on being there, ideally, at least forty minutes before the test starts. Remember, you have your Scantron and all of your materials ready to go in your backpack, so there's no need to stress out about that. All you're going to do now is pull out your review sheet and run through all of the concepts a couple more times.

Pick a place on campus somewhat near your classroom, but away from the action and not on the path toward the classroom, to do this review. You don't want to run into people from the class that might potentially ask you questions. This is a quiet time. You might even prefer to stay in your car to do this, assuming the parking lot or parking structure is close enough to the classroom.

Once you've found a decent spot, it's time to review. When you're reviewing, you want to keep it light. By this point, you know all of this stuff, and you're just reviewing to reactivate all of the mnemonic devices you've created for yourself and to take another glance at all of the learned knowledge you've acquired over the past week. Also, you want to look at these things and then realize, "Oh yeah! I know that!" That's all you're looking to do here.

The other benefit of a last-minute review goes back to "The Visual Technique" (Chapter 12.) You'll possibly be able to pull out a question or two on the test that you wouldn't have remembered otherwise just by remembering what the definition of the term looked like written down on your review sheet.

You only need to review this stuff on the review sheet a maximum of two times. Anything more than three is really overdoing it. During the first round, make this the round that counts, where you really reintegrate all of the concepts into your mind. Then, take a five-minute break. Eat your protein bar. Listen to a song. Soak in juicy, private conversations going on around you that you shouldn't be listening to.

Then, start the second round. During this round, let the focus be on reassuring yourself that you know the terms. Treat this second round just as a double-check. It should be really fast.

Become a Zen Master

At this point, you have about 15 minutes until showtime. Now's the time to take a couple minutes to relax and really get into the right mind state. You want to be relaxed, calm, and confident, with a hint of humor flowing through your veins. Don't stress out about the threat of becoming nervous during the test. You're well prepared for this test. It's time to show up and kick some ass.

The more relaxed you can stay, the easier it is to snap back into relaxed mode, and not fall into nervous mode. Take a couple of deep breaths, think about a calm atmosphere and what you feel like when you're happy, and relax.

After you feel good, get up, and go to the classroom or lecture hall. If you don't feel 100% calm yet, it's okay. Once you get up and start moving, you'll probably feel right a couple of minutes down the road. Remember, you're on a mission, and you're going to get in and out of this as efficiently and as easily as possible.

Can You Really Pull This Off?

Once you show up to the classroom, things get real. How many times have you been in class ten minutes before your test starts, and every **single** other person in the class is scrambling, looking at their notes, and asking questions to the other students in the class? I'm assuming your answer is *every time.*

Goddamn! No wonder everyone gets so stressed out during tests. Obnoxious people dump their own insecurities and poor planning on everyone else right before the test, and they make the test-taking environment a hostile, scary one for everyone who's trying to mind their own business.

Well, if you've been a part of that group before, which I'm sure all of us have at one point or another, it's time to kick back and relax, because we're going to remove that aspect of the test game completely out of the equation.

If you stroll over to the classroom before the doors have opened, it looks like a disaster outside of the room. People are camped out in front, frantically trying to compare notes with others, and they're reviewing like crazy! This can be a stressful thing to sit through, and it's no fun.

If you show up early, you'll be served an extra helping of this crap that you shouldn't have to eat. Chances are, all of these desperate clowns are going to rattle your cage a little bit. Doubt may rear its ugly head.

"Did I really study enough?"

"What are all these other people studying?"

"Should I have spent more time on 'Economies of Scale?' That's all these two guys have been discussing right next to me for the last ten minutes."

It's normal…shit, it's expected, to have these kinds of doubts. These people are messing with your nerves. Great. But, going back to the basketball example in the beginning of this chapter, are you going to be like LeBron, or are you going to be like Kobe?

Most of us have strived to have unwavering confidence our whole lives. But the first thing you've got to understand is this. Kobe has feelings too!

Do you think Kobe doesn't have thoughts like, "Oh shit, I wonder if Dwight Howard is going to hit me in the face when I go up to slam dunk the ball right now?" Of course he does! He's a human being. Everyone has hesitations, fears, and doubts. The difference is in the way you handle them.

LeBron gets nervous that he's not going to win the game. Instead of realizing that he's one of the greatest, if not **the** greatest, physical talent to ever play the game, he dwells on the fact that he's nervous. When it comes time to take a shot…"BOOM!" Brick.

Now let's talk about Kobe. There are two seconds left in a playoff game, and the ball is in Kobe's hands. If he misses the shot, his team loses the game. So, do you think he doesn't doubt and question what's going to happen? I guarantee you those thoughts run through his head. It's just that after those thoughts run through his head, he snaps into a more matter-of-fact attitude and decides, "You know what? I'm one of the best motherfuckers to ever play this game, and I'm taking this damn shot. I've made 'em before. Let's see what happens." Then, he's confident when he shoots the ball.

Here's another important point that I want you to pick up on. The shot goes in because he, just like LeBron, has the talent to make the shot. They both probably make at least 70% of their three-pointers during practice. Kobe wins, while LeBron gets widespread criticism, because Kobe's mental game is tight.

You've got the talent to score well on this test. You've studied, you've done the work, and you're ready to think on your feet. Now all you've got to do is shoot the ball.

For all of the effort you spend worrying, I bet you haven't taken the time before to actually answer those self-doubting questions that come up in your head.

As a solution to your stress, the next time you panic and question yourself, just let the questions flow out. Then, simply answer the self-doubting questions after. It's that simple. Give it some serious thought. Ask yourself the question.

"Have I studied enough?"

I bet you have. There's nothing to fear. So you can let go of being so on-edge about whether or not other people are going to make you freak out **about** being prepared.

Most of these people around you have **not** adequately prepared for the test. Those mad-rush questions you're overhearing from your peers, while they may freak you out and make you question yourself, are probably uneducated questions in the first place. If they were really ready for this test, they wouldn't be sitting around asking questions.

You've got this. Fuck what everybody else is doing. It might **seem** a lot more stressful and doubtful now that you're in the room with other people and everyone else is nervous, but the truth is, nothing's changed from five minutes ago when you felt ready and confident. Don't trust your judgment in regards to how well-prepared you are when you're riddled with anxiety. You knew you were ready when you felt confident before. It's still true when you're nervous.

Where Do I Sit?

So, when should you arrive in the classroom? You need to arrive about ten minutes early because you need to get a good seat position. You don't want to be in the front row of the test with the professor on your ass the whole time, and that's simply for the fact that you want no distractions. The distraction could be coming from your own imagination, if you're going to worry that the professor might think you looked at another person's paper. In any event, you don't need the headache. I would also recommend against sitting in the very back row, again, because the professor will assume those students are more likely to cheat and you'll become the subject of unnecessary scrutiny.

You also don't want to sit next to people that you know are going to be annoying during the test. That obnoxious kid with no social skills who always asks you about the Red Sox or your shady buddy who will inevitably ask if he can copy your answers are not the people you want to be around. This is a solo affair. You're getting down to business here. You're not here to make friends, or even to talk to anybody.

If you're in a class with some of your close friends that are cool, then that's fine, but if you have no close friends in the class, keep yourself isolated. Sit in a regular, inconspicuous seat, and, if possible, sit between two random people that look reasonable and calm. You should do this to avoid the shitty situation of having some asshole that smells or wheezes sitting down in an empty seat next to you two minutes after the test starts.

Also consider environmental factors. If you have an afternoon class, you don't want the sun shining on your face through an open window while you're trying to take the test. You also don't want to be burning up if it's 85 degrees outside, so, if that's the case, consider a seat near the air conditioning vent.

Here's another word to the wise. You know that hot girl or guy that you've wanted to talk to all semester? Today isn't the day to sit next to them. You're going to worry about your posture, if you're sweating during the test, if you look intelligent enough, and a myriad of other ridiculous topics if you sit near them. The worst is the, "I'm sitting next to this person. Should I actually turn my head and talk to them, or are they really not looking at me?" game. This is a distraction you definitely don't want today. Tackle this one on a random day when you would typically be skipping class. Go to the class, specifically, and exclusively, to talk to that person. It will be a lot easier that way.

What if Some Asshole Bothers Me Before the Test?

Inevitably, you're going to run into situations where someone wants to include you in their parade of shame. People who are irritating before tests are a lot like young children at the grocery store. Even though you don't want them there, they're everywhere, and they won't shut the fuck up. The objective here is to get them to fuck off as quickly as possible so you can focus on doing your own thing and not have to hear them talk anymore. The more shit they put into your head, the more you'll start questioning yourself. You've got a good thing going and a good vibe about yourself at this point, so you want them out of your hair quickly. Here's how to do it painlessly.

If They're a Friend:

Well, you don't want to be rude to a friend. In the situation I described above, if you feel like you're going to be distracted by your good friend that you normally sit with, then you need to sit in your own section. Say something like this to them:

"Hey girl! I'm doing this new thing for test focusing where I spend an hour by myself before the test and don't talk to anyone so I can focus on the material in my head. So when I come in the classroom, I'm just going to be sitting next to random people so I can knock out this test like a Tai Chi Master. But after, let's go get something to eat!"

This is easy to say, and it won't offend your friend. Just make sure that your message makes it clear that you don't see **them** as distractions, and that it's all about **you** working on improving **your** test skills.

This may not be enough for some friends though. They may want you next to them as a security blanket during the test, or they may start bitching about their own problems.

If they pull something like that, say:

"Well I didn't mean it like that, and I didn't mean to offend you obviously. It's okay. I can focus while sitting next to you. Just don't ask me anything about the test once we get in the room, because I'm going to handle all my reviewing ahead of time. Can you promise me that you won't do that?"

This should work. If they end up talking about the test anyway, just remind them that you're not participating in that conversation. Chances are, they'll respect your wishes.

If They're a Random Person:

As human beings, we typically don't care about random people as much. This is a good thing. Your well-being needs to be put on priority before a random person's today. At the same time, that doesn't mean that you need to be an ass and have a confrontational situation with the person you're sitting next to right before the test. If you do that, you run the risk of getting distracted by thoughts like, "Oh God, I wonder if I really pissed that person off?" during the test. That would blow.

Remember, the objective is for them to fuck off quickly without you being bothered during the process. So, if they ask you a question, here's the best thing to say:

Random Douche: *"Hey man, do you know what all of this stuff is about economies of scale? In page 348 of the text, it said that it's used in microeconomics, but I thought it was used in macroeconomics. In fact, I'm just confused all together. Did you take notes during class?"*

You: *"What's up dude. Honestly, I have no idea. I'm fucked for this test. I studied for like an hour this morning, and I haven't been showing up to class lately. You'd be better off asking someone else."*

This will get them every time. You're of no value to them if you don't know anything. This is the equivalent of a cute girl saying to a guy she doesn't like at a party, "Hey, I really like you, but I need to let you know something. I have three kids, and genital warts." The dude would be on his way in a second.

Sometimes, you'll get a real prick that will keep pushing it because he doesn't entirely believe you, or he might just not understand the concept of minding his own business.

Random Douche: *"Really? Wow, I can't believe you only studied for an hour. Well what's your plan for the test then?"*

Just keep giving short answers, and give them a blank look like you just got done smoking a lot of weed.

You: *"I don't know, man. I might transfer next semester. I've already got a 1.4 going into this semester."*

If they really won't stop, then after you're done explaining how you're not going to be able to help them, say, "I'm going to listen to my headphones now. Good luck." Then put your headphones on and turn away from them. That's all you have to do.

The beauty of this is that even though everything you've said is a complete lie, it doesn't matter. This clown doesn't have control over your grade. It doesn't matter what he thinks, as long as he fucks off.

Last-Second Mental Prep

Now that you're in your seat and actually ready to take the test, it's time to get your Scantron, pencil, calculator, and whatever else you need for the test. Put them on the corner of your desk.

As far as what to do now, you have a couple of options. It's ideal to spend about five minutes before the test taking a mental break. The best remedy for this, in your limited mobility, is to pull out the iPod and listen to a cool song. Listen to something immersive. Pick a pump-up song or something meaningful - anything that will completely captivate you. Don't worry about what you look like listening to music while everyone else is scrambling. They're the ones who look like idiots for still trying to study moments before the test.

If you really don't care what other people think, it will work best if you pull out some big noise-canceling headphones, like the Beats by Dre or the Bose QuietComfort15.

This works for a variety of reasons. For one, you'll be more immersed in the music because there's better sound on these types of headphones. Secondly, for your own sanity, it will get rid of the noise **completely** around you. If you close your eyes, you can imagine yourself anywhere, and you'll be totally zoned out from your surroundings for a few minutes. It's the best way to remove yourself from any situation that you have to be physically present for. The third benefit of noise-cancelling headphones is that when you wear them, you put a metaphorical **FUCK OFF** on your back, so other people won't ask you questions. If they try to ask you a question, they're just being rude, and you should completely ignore them.

If you're not into the music idea, pull out your smartphone and browse the net. Go on ESPN.com, or TMZ, or something else mindless that has nothing to do with the task at hand. Of course, if you have games, you can always play *Angry Birds* or something like that too.

If you don't have a smartphone, pack a magazine – again, something light and easy to read, like *Entertainment Weekly*, *Maxim*, or *Cosmo*. Any magazine with articles you can jump in and out of for a couple of minutes will work. Just allow your mind to naturally drift to something else and kick back. This is all going to be over soon.

CHAPTER 14

Taking the Test

All right, now you're past the mental pre-game warm up. It's time for the main event. The professor hands you your test. Now, what? Well, let's start by picking through it methodically.

Read Through the Entire Test Before You Answer Anything

Forget about the procedure that people typically follow, where you start on question one and work from there. We're going to attack things a little smarter than that.

The first thing you need to do, before you put down a single answer, is read over the entire test. You need to thumb through it for about two to three minutes and look at the format. You want to get familiar with this bad boy and understand what the test is going to be like.

It's here that you can actually relax a little bit more too. You're going to give yourself the opportunity to read over this whole thing, so there's no suspense. There won't be a scenario where you're turning the page after you're 10 questions deep, scared and wondering if that one question that you know you're going to screw up on is on the next page. It's all going to be laid out on the table ahead of time, before you even start.

Even if you discover that you're screwed and that, for instance, all of the stuff that you chose to skip studying is the main focus of the test, now you'll at least discover it at the beginning, and you'll be able to deal with it in a calm manner and come up with a plan of attack.

Read over all of the questions, whether it's multiple choice, short answer, essay, or a combination of all three, quickly. You should recognize the wording of most of the questions right off the bat due to your awesome study skill set and the recon work you did during the study guide/review lectures.

While you're thumbing through the test, this will also get you subconsciously thinking about the answers to these questions, almost like another quick review with your review sheet. However, this time, you're doing it with the real test!

You'll start thinking, "Oh yeah, I know that one, and, shit, I may have a little trouble on this next one." A word to the wise though – once you're actually ready to start answering questions, **make sure to read the questions completely**. Professors will throw in bullshit words like, "Which of these **don't** fit," that will throw you off when you're speed reading through them. We'll deal with this in depth in just a minute.

Another added benefit to reading the test ahead of time is that you might get a couple of questions answered for you. Oftentimes, the professor will define a term in the context of another question later in the test. Question 3 might be, "Economies of Scale is defined as what?" and Question 17 might start off with, "Since Economies of Scale is defined as a cost or a production advantage for a business when it grows in size..."

It probably won't end up being as blatant as this, but look for it. Just put an asterisk or star next to these related questions, and examine them later when you go through and answer the questions. You just racked up a few easy points.

Your Game Plan for the Test

Here's where the fun starts. Let's think back to our categorization of memorized and learned knowledge for a minute. The memorized knowledge is the stuff with a time limit on it. Since you're relying on your mnemonic devices to remember them, they are the most fragile and easiest to forget. At the same time, they're also "plug and play" type answers that you can just fill in quickly and move past. For both of those reasons, I recommend answering these questions first. Answering these questions is easy, mechanical, and instinctive.

When you start activating your deep mind power about halfway through the test with learned knowledge concepts, you're going to start feeling a little fatigued in the brain. When that happens, you're not going to be able to think as quickly and answer these questions as swiftly.

If there were any learned knowledge concepts that you gave up trying to learn and ended up using the memorization techniques on, those will probably be the first memorized terms to escape your mind, so do those first.

So, if you're skipping around frequently, you might be thinking:

"Well, I might answer Question 7 and then go straight to Question 20. How do I keep track of all this stuff?"

When you're going through the test for the first time and glancing at the questions, take your pencil and circle all of the easy or memorized knowledge questions on the printed test. A lot of professors will say, "Don't write on the test, or else." Fuck them. If you're circling lightly in pencil, you can easily go through the test after you're done and erase these marks.

After you knock out the memorized knowledge, the next thing you'll do is tackle the learned knowledge questions, and any other questions that you know you're going to have to think about to be able to answer. After that, it's essay time. Any extended essay questions that require longer than a three or four sentence response will be saved until the very end.

If you come up with specific concepts that you want to use on an essay question that you know you're going to forget, again, use your test as a piece of scratch paper. Jot down a few words when you first start about the concepts you want to use later, and focus on making it as succinct and clear to yourself as possible. Remember, no one is going to read this but you, so just be concerned with having your notes make sense to you. Later, you can come back and write the grand, full version of your essay. Just avoid writing an entire essay first when there's multiple choice questions left to be dealt with, because the essay will tire you out.

So, there's your game plan for the test. Answering the questions in this order will make things less stressful, and you'll never miss out on the easy points again. The learned knowledge questions, and the memorized knowledge questions that aren't so obvious, are always the ones that get people tangled up. Have you ever felt like you were on a roll, but then you ran into a couple of tough questions, lost your confidence and ended up boning the rest of the test?

Guess what? We've already solved that problem. We've already improved your score by answering all the easy "gimme" questions first, so now you don't have to worry about boning any questions you would have normally gotten right because you're angry, confused, or tired. It goes back to the philosophy of "racking up points." You've secured all of the easy points. Now all you have to do is not bone the harder questions.

What Do I Do With Impossible Questions?

First of all, you know you've studied adequately for this test. So, when one of these questions comes up that makes you question the existence of life itself because it's so complicated, chances are it was designed specifically to screw you. It's okay. Every test might have a couple of these questions, and you can't do anything about it, no matter how much you study.

If there's something that just seems completely ridiculous, then – you've guessed it – skip it until the very end. Leave the ones that are going to ruin your self confidence and make you feel like an idiot until the very end, even after the essay questions.

Let's be real here. If this question is causing you this much anxiety already, then the chances are low that you're actually going to get it right. So leave it until the end and consider it a bonus if you get it right.

The Multiple Choice Game

Luckily for you, with all of the mnemonic techniques we've used and all of the study prep you've put yourself through, most of the multiple choice questions should just be a snap. It should be, "I see it. I know the answer right away. Boom, I'm done. Perfect."

But you're always going to have those tricky questions on the test too. When you're irritated, what happens normally when you're answering a multiple choice question on a test? For most people, a thousand questions run through their minds, for the common goal of trying to find one simple solution.

"What's the fucking answer? Tell me!"

Your mind, as smart as it is, will try to come up with every possible scenario that will give you some sort of insight as to what the answer is. Most of the time, a lot of what you're thinking about has little to do with the content of the test.

It might be things like:

"Well, the last answer was 'B,' so this can't be 'B' too."

"I bet she's trying to screw us on this one, so even though it looks like 'C,' it should probably be 'A.'"

Even worse, once you get deeper into the test, you might start questioning your previous decisions during the test, and then try to balance them out by saying:

"Oh, well I just did two questions where I assumed they were trick questions, so I should probably just treat the next one like it's straightforward."

Then, before you know it, you're starting to calculate the probability of how many questions were straightforward and how many were trick questions. It's a dirty game! But unfortunately, you're going to have to navigate through your own conspiracy theories and come up with the right conclusions. Like the great Ice Cube said, "Pimpin ain't easy, but it's necessary."

There's no one-size-fits-all answer I can give you for exactly how to play this scenario out. Your ever-inquisitive mind is right sometimes. They are trying to screw you on some of these questions. But sometimes, you can overdo it, read into things too much, and then make up these conspiracy theories that are way off-base. Some experienced test-takers completely ignore answer patterns on the Scantron when selecting an answer.

There is one thing that you can always rely on to give you the **best** answers during this shitshow of a test. It's not going to be right 100% of the time, because you're not a robot, but the automatic go-to here is for you to trust your intuition.

You know how they say, "Trust your gut?" That's what we're going to do here. But don't get this confused with the intuition's little brother, the "First Instinct." If you read a question and something immediately pops out at you as the right answer, then that's great, and chances are, that may be the right answer. But, read it again and look it all over. Give it a good analysis. If it still looks right, then that's your answer.

If you have no idea whatsoever, then sure, go with that first instinct response. But the reason people say to "trust your first instinct" is because they don't want you to linger and make up ridiculous justifications for every other answer and get yourself all jumbled up. While that is good advice, if you can keep things calm and approach the question with a common-sense attitude, then you don't have to worry about that pitfall either. You can enjoy the added benefit of analyzing the other choices more without throwing yourself off. This will allow you to use both your instincts and your smarts. With everything working together, you'll improve the probability of getting the answer right past just what your "first instinct" is. It's the best bet, every time.

Another great technique that will make things less jumbled in your head is something that you may have learned already at an SAT Prep Class. If you have four or five choices, draw a line through the ones that you know are wrong. It helps visually, because you can take a blatantly wrong answer out of the picture. You're no longer staring at five possibilities, even though you consciously know two of them are wrong. You're only staring at three. It makes things simple.

I doubt I have to tell you this next part again because you could probably care less about the rules, but don't worry about making marks on the test if the professor said, "Don't write on the test!" You can easily erase this stuff if you make light marks. If they still complain after that, too bad. What are they going to do? Take off points on your test? If you get called out, just say, "I forgot."

"What if I Slip Into Overanalysis?"

If you find yourself slipping into overanalysis on a question and getting overwhelmed, the solution is actually really simple. All you have to do is take a quick break. Most people are so worried about finishing the test on time that they've assumed tests need to be one consecutive, hour-long mindfuck. This assumption couldn't be further from the truth. You really don't need to worry about getting into this overanalytical, overthought, overwhelmed mode, because all you have to do during the test is just back it up. Just slow down, and give yourself a break for a few seconds.

Sometimes, it's a little easier said than done to jump back into relaxed mode. You can get caught in a state of mind where you're nervous and you're too wrapped up in your emotions to think clearly. But if you give yourself thirty extra seconds and really just focus on turning your mind off – don't focus on making yourself relax, but focus on doing nothing - then you will come around, and you'll start to think clearly again.

Remember this simple piece of advice while you're taking the test. Everyone has thirty seconds. Even if you're pressed for time, thirty seconds is nothing. You can afford to spend that time to get yourself back into the right mind frame.

If you freak out once, and then you freak out five minutes later, just repeat the process with yourself. If it comes up again, keep doing it. After the third or fourth time, you'll realize how silly this back-and-forth game you're playing with yourself is, because your clear head is right there with your nerves, and you'll be able to drop the whole issue entirely.

However, on certain occasions when you're really freaked out, no matter what you do, you just won't be able to get yourself to calm down. That's fine. You've gotta play the hand you've been dealt. Remember, you're in here as a cold-ass ninja assassin who came to kill this test and get the fuck on. Even if you don't feel like a ninja assassin during the entire duration of the test, it's okay. No one feels confident all the time. Remember, even Kobe gets nervous.

What matters is getting this test done. You can still kill it even if you're nervous. Keep on trucking. Once you realize for yourself that you're still doing this, and you're still killin' it, even while you're feeling nervous as hell, your emotions have a tendency to calm down by themselves anyway.

Take Breaks Even When You Aren't Nervous

Even if you don't get nervous during the test, it's to your benefit to take breaks anyway. I'm not talking about taking a nap or getting up and going to lunch. I'm talking about a 30 second time-out where you allow yourself to take things down a notch and give your eyes a break.

Have you ever seen someone stop during the middle of a test to look up and stare at the wall? Probably not. Most people have their head buried in their desk the whole time like it's some sort of mental marathon. Give yourself a break.

Sometimes you just need to break up the momentum for a second to feel clear-headed again. Have you ever gotten lost while driving to a new place? Instead of stopping to reassess the situation, you just keep driving around for 20 minutes, aimlessly. You know that you should stop, spend the 30 seconds it takes to pull out your phone and look up directions, but you just keep going anyway. Then, eventually, you stop, you get the directions, and you're on your way.

Why do our brains work like this? You would have saved yourself 20 minutes of grief if you had just listened to yourself in the first place. Don't make that mistake when you start to feel flustered during a test. You need to stop the momentum of all this heavy material for a few seconds so you can feel refreshed. If you don't do it every so often, fatigue and irritation will accumulate.

No matter how tight of a schedule you're on with this test, you've got enough time for a few 30-second breaks where you can just catch your breath and even close your eyes if you want to. You've probably been too busy burying your head in your test all of these years to realize that you can afford the extra minute during an hour long test to do this. Sure, other people in the class might see you and say, "What the fuck is that guy/girl doing?" But so what? These people would be better off if they did it too, so screw them.

Dealing With Short Answer and Essay Questions

I know most people hate short answer or essay questions on tests. Personally, I kind of like them, and I enjoy them for a couple of reasons.

First, there's typically no bullshit associated with them. They ask you for information, and you give it. There's no mind games that they'll pull like they do with the multiple choice section.

Secondly, with a multiple choice question, you'll run into situations where you have to pick between two answers that are both technically right, and potentially end up getting the question wrong (and thus, zero points) even though you deserve to get the answer right since you know the material. With a short answer or essay question, you can get more of the points right if you demonstrate that you know what you're talking about, even if your answer is technically wrong. Professors are more lenient on short answer questions.

Lastly, my personal favorite reason for enjoying short answer/essay questions on the test is that you can easily bullshit your way through them if you know the right things to say.

Now, all of the principles that applied in Section 2 when we covered writing are the same here. Go back and read that again if you need a refresher course on how to write well for college. Remember, there are five main ingredients for a good essay:

The Five Key Ingredients for a Great Paper (Or In-Class Essay)

- ☑ **Ingredient #1: Throw in "Key Terms"**
  Include the terms and key buzz words that the professor wants to hear.

- ☑ **Ingredient #2: Give Them a Demonstration**
  Show the professor that you can define these terms. Demonstrate that you know what you're talking about.

- ☑ **Ingredient #3: Use Your "Grandma Voice"**
  Don't write the way you would normally speak in front of your friends while you're writing an essay. When you clean up your language, talk more formally, and speak in complete sentences, you're using your "Grandma Voice." Use this for your essays.

- ☑ **Ingredient #4: Add a Dash of Flair**
  Come up with ideas, arguments, and conclusions for your essay that will show your professor that you're thinking outside the box. Put your creativity on full display, and don't be afraid to share unique ideas, as long as they're not too over-the-top.

- ☑ **Ingredient #5: Refine Your Wording**
  Write in complete sentences, and make it sound like this essay was something that you were inspired to write. Make it seem like you actually thought about the creation of this essay and that it means something to you. Don't make it look like you just mechanically threw a bunch of scattered topics together.

Short Answer Questions

Let's deal with a short answer question first. We don't need to worry about Ingredient #4 for short answer questions normally. If they say, "Define economies of scale," what are you going to do? **Remember, your objective is to rack up points.**

Let's say this question is worth five points. To get the full five points, which you want to strive for on every question, you're going to need to describe accurately "economies of scale" in complete sentences. That's it. But, there are a few tricks of the trade that can make or break you here.

Don't Add Too Much Information

Let's say that you have a pretty good idea of what "economies of scale" is. You write two sentences about it, and it sounds like a pretty good definition. But, next, you want to add an extra sentence where you provide a real world example of a company that benefited from having growth, and exemplified the concept of "economies of scale." Good idea!

The problem is – maybe you're only about 70% sure that this extra sentence is right. You're worried that your example may not exactly coincide with the definition of "economies of scale." But the information in the first two sentences is gold.

Leave it alone! Don't add the example. You know why? Even though the first two sentences would have gotten you the full five points, if you add a third sentence that is just straight up wrong, then you'll lose points.

It isn't fair, because you included everything that was worth the five points, and tried to go above and beyond your duty to add more, but that's how professors play you. They will screw you on this, so watch out for it. If you have a decent-sized short answer that you're sure is right, stick with that instead of being bold and trying to go for more.

Write Properly

Write in complete sentences unless specifically directed by your professor to do otherwise. You can have the answer completely right, but if the professor sees it written in a bullet-point format instead of a sentence format, he might take away points.

Keep in mind that these short answer questions are completely subjective for the professor. He can take off points just because his ass itches at the time he's grading your paper. You want to give him absolutely no excuses to take points off your score.

Fill Up Space and Make It Sound Like You Know What You're Talking About

This especially applies if you don't know what you're talking about and need to bullshit a short answer question. Let's start by looking at two sample responses to the short answer question, "Explain the Four P's of Marketing."

Answer 1 - Place, Promotion, Price, Product.

Answer 2 - Throughout the past century, marketing experts have zeroed in on the four most crucial elements of the marketing mix. They span across the entire spectrum of the marketing world, and when applied properly, a marketer will be assured to cover all of their bases when it comes to focusing on the task at hand.

The first answer is actually right. Those are the "Four P's of Marketing." But, the guy who wrote this answer didn't read the damn question correctly, because it says to "**Explain** the Four P's of Marketing." It doesn't say, "**List** the Four P's of Marketing." So, even though he knows the material, he would get a 2 out of 5 or a 3 out of 5 at most on that question because he didn't pay attention. That's especially unfair because he had prepared properly for the test.

The second answer exemplifies how to make it sound like you know what you're talking about when you really don't know the answer. You'll notice that the actual Four P's are missing from the answer. This girl probably didn't remember what the Four P's were. So, instead of leaving the answer blank or giving up, she decided to make something up based on what she actually did know.

Believe it or not, you know more than you think about any topic you've been studying. Since "The Four P's of Marketing" is a pretty general and main concept in an introductory marketing class, this girl probably said to herself:

"Well, I don't remember what they are, but I remember it was really important and it's like the core of this marketing class. I also know that all recent marketing ideas have been invented in the last century, so I can start it with that and kind of make it sound like I know what I'm talking about from there."

Remember, your goal is to **rack up points**. Leaving the answer blank gets you a zero. Putting down some cute little answer that you think is funny as a desperate plea to get the professor to show mercy on you will get you a **zero**. Throw something out – anything - and you'll get some points. That second answer would have been awarded 3 out of 5 or even 4 out of 5 points in most instances. The writing style was great, and even though she didn't know what she was talking about, she wrote it in a manner that seemed like she was confident about the topic.

The professor might think, "Well, maybe she just got so caught up in writing this that she didn't even think to list the Four P's."

You have to write so confidently that the professor will think you're smart, and be forgiving. Of course, this game doesn't work 100% of the time, and if you did this for all ten short answer questions on the test, he would probably catch on. Nevertheless, you can rack up some serious extra points here if you pull this off right.

Essay Questions

The same rules we just went over apply for an essay question too, except we have to factor in Ingredient #4 now as well. The essay format typically calls for you to be more opinionated. The professor is looking for your specific insights and interpretations on the subject at hand in an essay, rather than just a definition. Of course, you'll be expected to define things too, but you'll also have to come to a conclusion in your writing and make it sound profound. Above all else, remember to sound like you know what you're talking about.

Don't Sound Like Too Much of a Smart-Ass

No matter how well you know this material, and how well you've studied for this test, your professor knows the material better than you do. You're going to get an "A" if you bring some interesting new light to the topic and write something that is really great. However, that doesn't mean that you need to act like a curator for a museum talking about a Van Gogh.

Unless you really feel like you're an absolute master of this material, don't go off on pretentious bullshit and aim for a super-creative higher-level conclusion. I'm not saying that you shouldn't be creative or strive to produce a thought-provoking conclusion. I'm just saying that if you go for literary-master-interpretation status, there's a high probability you'll just piss off your professor's ego.

You'll go, in their eyes, from a lowly student that can learn something from them, to some prick that they want to teach a lesson to. "How could he dare to bring into question something that I've spent years studying?" is something they might think. You don't want to put yourself into this situation, so find a happy medium.

In Class vs. At Home

The only other thing I want to stress here for an essay during a test situation is that it's really not any different than writing a paper at home. One main thing you need to keep in mind is to not rush through it or let the pressure get to you. Relax. You can write this in the allotted time. You can't dilly-dally with the in-class essays, because the professor won't typically give you an abundance of time, but make sure to keep things calm inside yourself. Your writing process will be no different than it is at home.

Start with the outline, and then write. If possible, get rid of, scratch out, or throw away your outline after you're done so that the professor doesn't see it. We don't want him judging you on a rough draft. After you get a solid outline down, flesh out the paragraphs and your conclusion, and you'll be done before you know it.

Also, don't worry about scratching out a mistake or a misplaced sentence. The goal is for this thing to be as easy as possible for the professor or TA to read. A blacked-out line in pen is a lot better than a "carrot" with an extra sentence written in-between two lines. Be sure to write legibly.

Keep reminding yourself to maintain a slow and steady pace. You know all of that extra time that you think you're saving by rushing and writing fast? That actually totals up to an extra minute or two over the course of the entire essay-writing process. It doesn't pay to be panicked, even when you're in a hurry.

Have you ever noticed that you can walk a mile in ten minutes, but if you huff and puff and run a mile, you end up doing it in eight minutes? How does that make sense and how is that fair, when you put so much more effort into running? Think about that. Walk the mile when you're writing an essay. You'll do yourself a huge favor.

Time Management for Test Taking

This is a perfect time to move into a quick sub-section on time management. Remember, you will have more time than you think. All you have to do is plan ahead. The professor will always tell you before the test starts, "You have one hour to complete this test," or whatever. When you start your routine of going through the questions, begin taking inventory.

"How many multiple choice questions are there?"

"How many essay questions are there?"

These are obvious questions, but you need to think about them. Let's say you have twenty-five multiple choice questions and one essay question, with an hour to do the test. You need to play to your strengths.

Look at that essay question. Is it an easy topic that will be no problem for you to knock out, or is it going to be your main struggle?

Are these multiple choice questions mostly memorized knowledge, "gimme" questions?

Does writing come naturally to you, or are you more comfortable with multiple choice?

Break it down. Decide what's going to be easy, and what you're going to need more time on. Then, give yourself multiple "deadlines," which should serve only as guidelines. Let's say you decide to spend 20 minutes on the multiple choice, 30 minutes on the essay, 5 minutes for checking your answers and answering the "impossible"-type questions, and 5 minutes for "extra time." This "extra time" can account for mental breaks, as well as more time to complete one of the sections in case you run over. I would always recommend giving yourself an "extra time" cushion, because it takes the pressure off.

Now that the general plan is here, get going. You'll be able to tell once you get into the multiple choice section whether or not you're on pace. But, remember to make these things semi-deadlines. You're going to need that 30 minutes for the essay. So, if you're 15 minutes into the multiple choice section and you've only got half of it done, then you need to pick it up. You don't want to leave yourself out to dry with the other section.

Again, with multiple choice, we're saving the hardest, lowest-probability-of-getting-it-right questions for the end anyway, so if you end up not getting to those, it's not as bad as missing a couple of the "gimme" questions.

But, even when you plan it out and everything looks like it's going to work, there will be times when you're behind schedule and you're going to have to rush. When this comes up, what should you do? I hope, "Relax" was the first answer you thought of. Sure, you're not going to get things perfect like you would if you had an extra hour to complete the test. But you do have **some** time left.

Charge It To the Game

One of my favorite sayings is, "Charge it to the game." The rapper Silkk Tha Shocker from No Limit Records even had a CD titled that. What does it mean? It literally means to charge your situation to a metaphorical credit card, and you can afford to do so because you're rich in life skills. But, in layman's terms, it means, "Fuck it. This situation sucks. But I'm going to make the best of it, keep it moving, and enjoy the fact that I don't have to let this situation rattle me, even though I've gotten screwed."

If you go to a baseball game and they charge $12 for a beer, what are you going to do? You're not going to **not** have a beer. You're going to get it. But you got screwed. Charge it to the game.

Some asshole rear-ended your car in the parking lot while you were at the grocery store, and they left without writing a note. Charge it to the game. Your friend's dad is a mechanic and can fix it for free anyway.

This is the mind state you need to be in when the shit hits the fan and you have only a few minutes left to write an essay. It's not going to be perfect, but you can still get it done. You'll be ineffective if you wrap yourself up in "how fucked you are right now." But, if you can take humor in the fact that you are fucked, even though you know you still have to perform, situations like these will become a lot easier than you think. It will allow you to keep moving and actually get things done. If you sit around and dwell on the fact that you're screwed, you'll **be screwed**. But if you can "charge it to the game," you'll be able to regain your composure and give it your best shot when you get into sticky situations.

Checking Over Your Test and Turning It In

Here's where all of you overanalysts will start freaking out again.

"Should I check over all of my answers before I turn it in?"

"What if I had it right the first time and I end up overanalyzing things and screwing it up?"

Don't worry. You're not going to sabotage yourself unless you allow dumb thinking on your part to make a final decision – and that's exactly what happens when you get overwhelmed and try to change things in a rush at the end. Instead, as we have during this entire test, we're going to take a controlled, easy approach.

Here's the solution to your overanalysis first. You already did all of the analysis, played all of the mind games, and did all of the complicated thinking when you were actually answering the questions. So, leave it at that, and don't even revisit the tricky questions when you're checking over your test. There is an exception, though.

For those questions where they play wording games like, "Which of these is **not** an example of depreciation?" read those again. You want to make sure you didn't make a dumb error and accidentally answer which one **was** an example of depreciation. And if you thought it was hard to follow the last couple of sentences, that's just another argument for why you should always re-check these types of test questions.

For everything else, leave it alone. Use the review as a time where you double check that the right answer that you picked corresponds to the same answer that's filled in on the Scantron. Also make sure that there are no blank answers on your Scantron. That's all you really need to be doing.

Obviously, while doing this, if you notice something that you screwed up on, then be sure to fix it. I just don't want you to re-think the entire test here.

If you have short answer or essay questions, then proofread them very quickly and make sure that there are no silly mistakes like missing words or misspellings. Chances are, there will be very few errors. If you've been running through this the way it's been laid out here, you did a very thorough job, and you can pat yourself on the back.

The other benefit of checking this stuff over is that it can give you the mental reassurance that you really got the answers right. That feeling will tide you over until your test score comes in later. It's the same sensation as double-checking that your door is locked at night before you go to sleep. It just feels good.

You know what to do from here. Get up. Get your materials while making sure that it doesn't look like you're trying to put anything suspicious into your backpack. Give your professor a wide-eyed, happy smile. Say, "Thank you." Hand him the test, your Scantron, and any other materials.

Walk out the door. Exhale. Now go out and do whatever the fuck you want to. You just got the damn thing done, and you did it in a way that is guaranteed to improve your GPA. It's time to celebrate.

CHAPTER 15

Extra Questions You May Have Regarding Tests

As you know, not every aspect of your life will work completely around a perfect schedule. For that reason, I've included an extra chapter where you'll find solutions to many common situations you may face during the hours leading up to the test.

"What if I Have to Cram the Night Before the Test?"

If, for whatever reason, you fell into a bad spot and you know you're going to be up until 3 a.m. studying the night before the test, it's still possible to be successful in your studying and to get a good grade. But let me make this clear – it's not going to be as comfortable.

What I spent the last two chapters walking you through is like the Four Seasons version of test-taking prep – the ideal, luxury version. You're about to embark on the Motel 6 version. The basic principles still apply here, but don't expect things to be as pleasant.

First off, acknowledge that you need at least five hours of sleep to be minimally efficient the next day. You're pushing it at four hours, and if you get three or less, you might as well just forget it.

Remember, even if you're studying until 3 a.m., you need to abide by the same guidelines that I've outlined in the previous chapters. If you find yourself losing focus, you need to take a break. Unfortunately, when it gets to be 1 a.m. and you've been reading for five hours straight, these situations are going to appear in a higher frequency.

"So, how do I counteract a lack of focus?"

The first impulse for many of us is to drink a Red Bull or a coffee. I would recommend against this though, unless you're a veteran caffeine drinker and know exactly how your body reacts to these drinks. If you normally don't drink this type of stuff, taking a Red Bull at 1 a.m. is going to torpedo you because you're not going to get any sleep when you finally end your studying at 3.

If you insist on energy drinks, then go for Red Bull or Monster, or any of the actual "drink" ones, and stay away from 5-Hour Energy. I have no idea what's in that stuff, but it's a different type of buzz that is designed solely to keep you awake, and it doesn't have the "pump-up" type buzz that you'll get from the caffeine-based drinks. Also, you **will not** fall asleep for five hours after taking one of those 5-Hour Energy drinks. It's definitely possible to fall asleep after a Red Bull or a coffee, but you'll have no such luck with that other crazy shit. You've been warned.

Anyway, I'm sure you've had long nights where you come back from some hardcore drinking at 2 or 3 a.m. When you come home, and you've got nothing to do the next day, you say to yourself, "Well, you know what? I normally get up at 8, but since I stayed out 'til 2 tonight, I'm not going to get up 'til 10 or 11 tomorrow." You simply shift the time you get up to a couple of hours later. You lose an hour or two of sleep, and although you're a little sluggish, you're fine the next day (assuming you're not terribly hungover.)

The same thing applies here. If at all possible, sleep later the next day, and give yourself as close to the golden-standard 8 hours of sleep as possible. If you have a class early the next day, skip it, even if attendance is required. Your mental health for this test is more important than one stupid attendance grade.

The bottom line is, you're not Superman or Wonder Woman. You can't do **everything,** and you're going to get tired. Don't let sleep or taking care of your body be the thing that takes the hit because you've planned this poorly. Your body will end up winning that battle by being a passive-aggressive little bitch the next day. Let your other plans suffer because of it instead, and the odds for your success with the test will be more in your favor. I've consulted a doctor on this matter, and the advice I was given is that **some sleep,** even if it's just an hour, is better than **absolutely no sleep.** Good luck, and Godspeed.

"If I'm Going to Cram, but Get Too Tired, Should I Just Spend More Time Studying the Day of the Test?"

Absolutely. You just need to allow yourself enough time in the morning for a study session where you actually learn the material, for a break (and that break could even be driving or walking to campus,) and for your last-minute review session.

If you don't have enough time in the morning to study, consider getting up early. For most people, getting up early is easier than staying up late and waking up on minimal sleep. If you're a part of this crowd, you can go to sleep at midnight and then get up at 6 a.m. to give yourself a couple more hours than you would have had the night before. That's manageable. It's not going to be perfect, but the easier you can make things on yourself, the better.

"What If I Have Multiple Tests in One Day?"

This will definitely happen from time to time, and when it does, it sucks. Remember to "charge it to the game." This is the hand you've been dealt. You can do it. Hopefully, the tests are at least an hour apart. If they're back to back, you're going to have to use your 10-15 minute break in between to go over your review sheet for the next test. I'd recommend eating that protein bar and having a glass of water during this time as well.

It's going to be a tight schedule, but as long as you can maintain your focus and realize it's going to be a long haul, you'll do fine.

Section 5:
Extra Credit

Congratulations! You made it through your assignments and your tests. You've got all of the tools you need to be in the top tier of your college class now. For the final section of the book, let's have some fun. The following quick little chapters will improve your overall college experience. Enjoy.

CHAPTER 16

Fun Games to Play During Class

Obviously, if you're stuck in a mandatory attendance class you don't want to be in, your best option is to pull out your laptop, connect to the free Wi-Fi, and browse the Internet during the lecture.

There is a bit of a science to this, though. If you're using a laptop during class, the assumption is that you're actually paying attention to the lecture, and that you're just using the computer to take notes.

For that reason, whether you're watching Youtube videos on mute, or updating your Facebook status, make it a point to look up at the professor every minute or so for a few seconds, and then type (or even fake type) on your computer after. This will maintain the appearance that you're using the laptop for legitimate purposes, and your chances of getting called out during class will be slim.

Also remember to keep a bored, uninterested look on your face. Think about it - that's what you would naturally look like if you were sitting through this drivel and actually paying attention. Sadly, the professor expects this. It ends up being another sign to them that you're actually listening.

If, for whatever reason, you don't have a laptop, I've included three of my favorite games that you can play discreetly with your friends during class. Sometimes, you'll find that playing silly games like these is even more fun than browsing the Internet.

The Hilarious Lyrics Game

My friend Cody and I invented this game during a shitty Economics class we took together sophomore year. Basically, it goes like this. You take a piece of scratch paper out during class and write down hilarious and/or filthy lyrics from a song that you've remembered, followed by the artist's name. The more outrageous the lyrics, the better time you'll have. For instance, I would write down this:

> "I met this MILF at the All-Star, gettin' action/A cougar with more rings than Phil Jackson." – Kanye West

Then, my friend takes the pen and paper and tries to top my selection with the best lyric he can think of. He would write:

> "Urine in your face, 'cause you're fake." – Eminem

As the game continues, it gets more and more difficult to refrain from bursting out into laughter during the middle of the lecture. That's part of the challenge. You want to keep a straight face and make it look like you're paying attention, when really all you can think about are the funny song lyrics.

Not a music fan? Then do it with movies! You can choose from thousands of one-liners from your favorite comedies. When that gets old, start going for some hardcore Joe Pesci lines from *Goodfellas* and *Casino* that are too gangsta to pass up.

Before you go hogwild with this, I'll offer one word of caution. You definitely don't want to get caught. Make the priority on having a good time here rather than pushing the limits. You don't want it to seem like you're passing notes. It's best when you're writing this stuff to do it on a random page in the back of a notebook that you move back and forth. This way, in case of emergency, you can just turn to a different page, and the professor will never find it.

The Story Game

This is also great for endless hours of entertainment. It's similar to "The Hilarious Lyrics Game," but it takes longer per round, and there's virtually no way to get caught.

The premise is simple. Pick any person you don't personally know in the class (I highly recommend the professor, but any random person is fine) and then write a page-long story about what that person did last night. If you haven't guessed already…yes, the goal is to make it as stupid and disgusting as possible. Here's a sample of what I'm talking about:

Last night, Professor Johnson decided to try his luck at cards. He headed out to one of those Indian casinos and hit up the blackjack table. Three Appletinis and five minutes later, he was about 100 dollars in the hole. He decided cards weren't going to be his thing tonight. But Johnson wanted to spend the 300 dollars he had left in his pocket. He wanted it gone by the end of the night. Luckily enough for him, the answer as to what he was going to spend it on appeared right in front of him.

7 foot 2, 350 pounds, with a fake leather coat and leopard print pants, this beast queen was the type of gal that Professor Johnson had been dreaming about for years. Mrs. Johnson couldn't satisfy him in the bedroom as of late, and he'd been looking to fuck around for a while. This could be his chance.

Wild Princess stared right at him and licked her lips. "She's DTF for sure. She likes my corduroy jacket," Professor Johnson thought. But there was a caveat. She made a gesture in the other direction, right at a later-day

Burt Reynolds-looking cowboy and the Tibetan Monk on his arm. "Really? A four-way? A guy doesn't get this lucky every day," Johnson thought. He looked over at the nasty duo, and they knew right away what was up.

The four of them headed to Wendy's on the way back to Johnson's place for a late night snack. They needed some food, because it was going to be a long night. "Hey Johnson, can you get this? I lost a lot of money at the casino tonight," said the Cowboy. Johnson paid for everyone's food. They sat down and shared a few laughs over 99 cent chicken nuggets. "Well, let's head back to my place now," Johnson said as he stood up. He then felt the cold sensation of metal on the back of his neck.

"Not so fast, motherfucker," said the Monk, armed with a .44 Magnum. "We're The Redemption Crew. You really thought we wanted to share our love with you? You're a buster. We use chumps like you every night to get free food. Cleomonstra over there entices you with her irresistible sex appeal, while me and the Cowboy over here are the icing on the cake. Now, lights out, bitch."

With that, he pistol whipped Professor Johnson. As he fell to the floor, blood oozed out of his neck. The Redemption Crew stole his car, and headed off into the night, never to be heard from again. This morning, Professor Johnson had to take the bus to campus.

Write something like that, and pass it to your friend. Your friend can then try to write their own Professor Johnson story, or pick another person. Changing up the style in which you write the stories might make it even more fun for you. Write some of them like a murder mystery novel, write some like a news article, and write some like a comedy.

You might notice that the above story was pretty terrible, quality-wise. That's the point. I just did that in one take without even thinking about it or making it perfect. This is a cool game for you to play, because it will also give you practice in the art of bullshitting. If you can come up with a creative story about a random person you don't know from class off the top of your head, that's a great talent to have, and you'll be able to apply it to your writing assignments later down the line.

The other reason why this is such a great game to play during class is that it's completely engrossing. When you're writing and actively thinking about creating a story, you won't get bogged down by the professor's boring lecture, or negative thoughts from your own mind about how much you hate the class. You can completely tune out when you're writing these things. And, hey, it also looks like you're writing notes while you're making your story up. The professor will never question you if you're actively writing during class. It just looks like you're doing work.

The Staring Game

This one's pretty self-explanatory. Pick a random person sitting in front of you, and have your friend monitor the clock. Your job is to stare blankly - completely stone-faced - at the back of this person's head, for as long as it takes until they notice you. The winner of the game is the person that can go the longest without having the random person turn around and notice them. If none of the random people catch on, you might need to try someone closer in proximity to where you're sitting. The winner, after however many rounds you decide to play for, gets free lunch after class!

Try it Out!

Experiment with these games, and put your own spin on them to make them your own. The point is to do something - anything - that will get your mind off of class if you've already made the decision not to pay attention. Have fun!

CHAPTER 17

How to Sound Like You Know What You're Talking About During Class

If you're screwing around during class, there will inevitably come a time when you get called on to answer a question and you have absolutely no idea what's been going on during the lecture.

If you're hoping to learn a magic trick here that will make words spew out of your mouth like a scholar, I can't offer that. But, I can offer you a quick how-to on where to get these words and how to speak them with confidence.

First, no matter how deep you are into whatever you're doing with your friends during the lecture, make it a point to stop for about 10 seconds every two minutes. Listen to what the professor is saying, and pick out key words and phrases that sound like they would be important. You don't need to understand what's being taught, or understand the context in which these words are being used. All you need to remember are the words. You can even write them down if you want.

Now, if you get called on, also keep in mind that you don't even have to give an adequate answer. If you use those words and phrases that you've picked out in a sentence of some sort, then it will sound like you were paying attention, at least to some degree. The professor might think you're an idiot, but you can save yourself from being on their shit-list by doing it this way. Your only objective is to throw out words that make it sound like you were at least somewhat paying attention. That's all you want. Go for the bare minimum.

How you speak when you're called on is the other side of being able to pull this off correctly. Your nervousness from knowing that you're clueless about the content of the lecture and your fear of impending embarrassment could just as easily be confused for you being shy and uncomfortable in front of crowds. So, luckily for you, you really don't need to be worried about that aspect of your delivery.

Here's where you can improve your speaking style. When you speak in slow, calm sentences, it sounds like you're more confident. Think about someone who has been paying attention this whole time. How would they speak if they were called on? They would respond a lot more casually and a lot more freely than someone who was trying to bullshit their way through a sentence. Even though you are trying to bullshit your way through this, if you sound like someone from the "I was paying attention" group, then you'll get pegged as someone who's been listening to the lecture and has been doing their job.

If all else fails, utter these magic words:

"I don't know."

The key is to not be sorry about it. Don't be embarrassed and break eye contact like a shamed dog after he ate food off of your plate. Just say, casually, "I don't know," or "I'm not sure." Say it like you would if your roommate asked you where your friend went, and you genuinely didn't know.

Try it in the mirror a couple of times.

"I don't know."

Your objective is to get the professor off your ass as quickly and painlessly as possible. So, even if you say, "I don't know," and they want to dig into you, as long as you keep saying, "Well, I don't know," in response, it exterminates the fire in a way.

If you keep responding shortly and don't look embarrassed, they won't have much they can do as far as humiliating you or making an example out of you. It's the people that look weak and want to try to get the professor's approval that end up getting ripped on.

If they keep pushing the issue, they may ask something like, "Well, why don't you know? Have you not been paying attention?" Just say in response, "You know what, I'm sorry, but I've had a rough day and I must have not been paying attention." You don't want to clown on them by coming up with some sassy, sarcastic remark, and you also don't want to make it a contest. Just keep it simple and short, and they'll fuck off soon.

CHAPTER 18

How to Beg, Plead, and Lose All Integrity So You Can Get a Better Grade

So, you've slaved your way through History 104, and after following the advice in this book and figuring out how to score better on tests, you end up doing great. You get your final grade and it's an... 89.7%

What? Goddamnit! There's nothing worse than getting screwed out of an "A" by less than half of a percentage point.

Once again, we're stuck in a predicament where your fate lies with an unreasonable bureaucrat who cares more about the fact that, "I don't round up – it's listed in the syllabus," than the fact that this technicality could potentially make or break your chances of getting into grad school.

I'm sure you know better than to buy into the bullshit they'll feed you.

"Well if you got an 89.7, then that's 'B'-quality work, and you deserve a 'B.'"

You deserve an "A." You deserve that grade. 0.3% is literally no difference. But to have a chance of getting the "A" that you deserve, you need to keep tabs on your professor from the beginning of the semester.

If you went to get a massage, and the masseuse charged 100 dollars an hour, wouldn't you feel gypped if they stopped after 55 minutes? You would want to milk them for every single second you paid them for. You need to treat your relationship with your professor the same way when it comes to your grade. Never, **ever** let even a single point slip away. If one homework assignment is missing, one class attendance grade isn't marked, or one short answer question on a test should have been awarded an extra point, always let them know immediately, and make sure it gets changed.

They'll be lazy about it, and they'll drag their feet in every way they can in most instances. But, if you make it less of a hassle to change your assignment score than to deal with your constant pestering, they will do it. If you have to, e-mail them three times a week about it, and keep repeating this until they change it. Keep these e-mails in a special folder within your e-mail account so you can have easy access to prove that you've discussed this with them earlier in the semester. This way, they can't lie later and say that they never received any communication about the issue.

Why should you be such a dick to the professors, and why should you be so anal about this? Because you won't get any love back at the end of the semester/quarter when you actually need that extra point. Let's say you have that 89.7% and, going back through your grade, you noticed that an attendance grade was missing for a class that you know you attended. If that grade were counted, it would bump you up to an "A." When you e-mail them at the end of the semester and inform them of this, they might say something like, "Sorry, but you should have disputed this earlier in the semester. It's too late now."

Trust me, this happens all the time. The professor's game is always to say that it's "out of their hands," or "it's too late," when that's complete fiction. All they have to do is load up Microsoft Excel and make a simple adjustment. If they can, they also love to say, "I would have changed it, but the final grade has already been sent in to the university." Don't believe that either. The grade can be changed once it's submitted to the university, even if it isn't changed until the next semester. To avoid this bullshit entirely, as soon as you notice a problem, you need to e-mail your professor right away.

But let's say, worse-case scenario, that it is the end of the semester already. If you need to change your grade at the end of the semester, remember that every hour matters here. Even though it's still possible to get a change in once the professor officially turns the grade in to the university, he won't want to put in the extra effort to get it changed at that point. Your probability of getting it changed is much greater if you can catch him before the grade is turned in.

For demonstration purposes, let's also say that you don't have a legitimate claim to a better grade, like a long-lost attendance grade. You just straight up scored an 89.7% in the class. What do you do?

Well, you still deserve the better grade. So, first, look for any easy outs that you can use. Even if your attendance grade is correct, look at the attendance scores if your class has mandatory attendance, and also look at cheap little homework assignments. Those can easily be mishandled, and it's plausible to believe that they just missed one of those. If you don't have any missing attendance or homework grades, you're going to have to grasp at straws. Look at assignments like a paper or a group project where the grade is subjective. Could there have been a reason to get a couple of extra points on one of those?

If you're going this far, your reasoning for getting a better grade is flimsy at best. So, it's time to put on your best ass-kissing face and get ready to throw a Hail Mary.

Before you start kissing ass, let me clarify something. **Don't expect that you'll get your grade changed even if you employ these techniques like a pro. Most professors are real assholes about this stuff.**

So, let's talk about ass-kissing theory. Most people don't like having their ass kissed, per se. They want to have their ass kissed, sure, but they don't want it to feel like an ass kissing. They want a gentle ass kiss to come from a person that they can respect as genuine, so it feels like it's worth something.

Keeping that in mind, you can blur the fact that you're basically pleading for their mercy and that you're willing to kiss their ass by keeping the tone of your begging e-mail honest and humble. You want to sound like a straight shooter who really deserves a better grade (at least in the first e-mail.) It should go something like this:

Hi Professor Johnson,

My name is AssKiss Murphy, I'm a student in your History 104 class (Monday Wednesday 4 p.m. Section 420.) I hate to bother you so late in the semester, but I'm having an issue with my final grade. As you can see, I scored an 89% on my final, which I'm very proud of, but unfortunately I just fell short of the required 90% to get an "A" in your course. I'm currently at an 89.7%.

I went through the rest of the semester's grades to see if there were any errors. I noticed that I had received a zero on the homework assignment from 10/24, and I'm not sure why this is the case, because I know I did that assignment. I'm glad I checked this, because with that homework in there, I would have enough points for an "A!" What's your policy on this? I wish that I could bring the actual paper in for you to see, but obviously all of the homework is in your possession.

Thanks for your time,

AssKiss

Now, notice how there's no sarcastic language in here, and there's no anger. Take on the mind-set that you're going to get what you want already, and assume it's going to happen as you're writing the e-mail. That's what would be fair if you actually did the homework assignment, right? Even if there are other policies like, "There are no grade changes at the end of the semester" in the syllabus, just ignore that at first, and make the professor be a dick if he or she is going to go that route in their response e-mail.

Also take note of the fact that there's no "demanding" type language in the e-mail. Don't put something like, "Let me know when it's changed, thanks." They don't like to be told what to do. Let the implications do the talking.

You might be done after this, and if that's the case, awesome. Send them another e-mail saying how much you appreciate it, and then that's that. Save a copy of the e-mail though. If they don't change your grade, you don't even need to bother with them again. Go straight to the Ombudsman or the Dean of Students with a copy of this e-mail and let them deal with it next semester.

But you might not be done. Here's a sample response e-mail:

> Hi AssKiss,
>
> Thanks for your interest in your grade. Unfortunately, I have a policy, which was explicitly written in the syllabus, that all grade disputations need to take place before the end of the semester. I don't have the record of you having completed this homework assignment, and I'm sorry that you were so close to getting the grade you were looking for. It's just not fair to the other students if I let this slide. Have a great winter break.
>
> -Professor John "ISuckDickOnWeekendsOnly" Johnson

This is par for the course. Now, for most people, this would be the end of the road. But, since you're almost done with this book by now, I hope you realize that you're not most people, and I hope I've ignited the fire inside of you so that you won't stand for bullshit like this. It's time to pull out a different method. In this next e-mail, you'll want to come off as an irrational person.

Here's an example that will explain what I mean. I love using this approach when asking for refunds from stores where I shop. I order furniture online, and one time I received a bookshelf that was supposed to be new, but had a slight dent in it. It had clearly been used before. I could have kept the bookshelf and it wouldn't have been a problem, but I had an issue with the principle of paying full price for a used bookshelf. So I called customer service.

The obviously-outsourced customer service agent answered the phone and I explained the issue. I said, "What can be done?"

The agent said, "Well, unfortunately this bookshelf didn't ship out from our warehouse. It came from a different location, so we don't have any more units. I could e-mail you a shipping label and have you send it back for a refund."

I didn't want a refund though. I wanted to keep the bookshelf, and get it for a discounted rate. So I just kept repeating myself. I said, "Well, this is damaged. This is a used bookshelf!"

He asked again if I wanted to get a refund by shipping it back. I said, "I don't want to go through the hassle of shipping it back out. This is a damaged bookshelf, and I mean, I guess I could use it, but it's not worth my time to ship it back."

He said there was nothing else he could do. Then I asked to speak to his supervisor. The supervisor came on the phone and I repeated the same words. "This is a used bookshelf! This is damaged!"

I pretended like I didn't understand why shipping it back for a refund was reasonable. Of course, I understood what they were suggesting, but I was acting like a moron so I could get what I wanted. You have to abandon your smarts sometimes to get what you want.

Think about what would happen if you're taking care of a child. They'll keep screaming, "I want candy now!" You can use all of the smarts and bargaining tactics you want to on them, offering them fruit snacks instead, offering to take them to the movies instead, or even offering candy after dinner. But no. They'll keep screaming, "I want candy now!" After going back and forth, your frustration will sink in, and you just give them the candy to get them to shut the fuck up.

Back to the bookshelf example, after going back and forth and just maintaining my stance, I got it for half off. That's what I wanted, and that's what I got. You just have to be willing to commit to it, and be willing to look like an idiot.

It's time to follow this format in your next e-mail response. Write something like this:

Hi Professor Johnson,

Thanks for replying. I just don't get why I can't get the grade that I actually earned in this class. Why does this policy exist? I didn't have time to look at my grade during the semester because I was without Internet to access my grade online for a couple of months. I have the points available to get the grade. I don't understand why this isn't fair to other students. This grade is going to determine whether I get into grad school next year, and I actually deserve this grade. That's the whole thing. I'm not asking you to change the grade. I'm asking you to just make the grade the way it should be. I know you're busy and I appreciate you taking the time out of your schedule to fix this error. Let me know what I can do to facilitate this process and I'll be available to help. Thank you.

-AssKiss

Now you've basically shown that you're ignorant as to why his policies are relevant, and you're calling a spade a spade by saying, "Hey, damnit, I got an 'A' so give me an 'A!'"

But, as much as you try, you can't expect this to work all the time. You might get a response like this:

> Hi AssKiss,
>
> The policy is in place because the university mandates that we lay out a list of rules in a syllabus. This is really for your own good.
>
> These rules need to be abided by the entire semester. I'm sorry to hear about the grad school stuff, there's just nothing that can be done at this point.
>
> -Professor John "IDoAnalOnSundaysToo" Johnson

If you get to this point, your chances of getting the grade changed are pretty slim. You could try to get the Dean of Students or the Ombudsman involved, but if you're lying about an assignment or attendance grade, then it's not worth it. Unfortunately, professors do hold power over you, and they can basically do whatever they want to when it comes to your grade. It sucks, but it's part of the game.

At the same time, don't let this motherfucker and his policies get you down. Just because he's repeating a policy doesn't mean that the policy is right to begin with. Even if he technically "wins" this battle while you lose, you'll win over time if you keep questioning bureaucratic policies and keep standing up for yourself. You don't need to accept his view of "what's right."

Final Words

Congratulations! You made it all the way through. I hope that you picked up on the general take-home message here. You can do college your way, on your own terms, and bypass other people's bullshit to make your own life easier.

What are you going to do with your newfound free time?

Go out and get drunk?

Work out?

Watch more TV?

I'm sure that it's going to be a combination of all those things.

I want to finish this book on a slightly sentimental note. Once you've been unplugged from the grind of bullshit schoolwork for a while, you might find that, since you're not learning what other people are forcing you to learn, there is some stuff out there worth learning on your own terms.

Now of course you're not going to love everything in the world. But maybe you've always wanted to learn how to skateboard. Maybe you've wanted to learn about psychology. Maybe you've wanted to learn how to cook. If you discover these types of callings, pursue them. That's the whole purpose of freeing up your time and your mind from bullshit throwaway classes. It gives you time to pursue what you really want instead.

Don't let the old notion that "learning is bullshit" hold you back. There's a quote from Mark Twain that I read recently in a business book called *Rework* by Jason Fried and David Heinemeier Hansson that fits perfectly here.

"I have never let my schooling interfere with my education."

What a dope quote. Enjoy your college experience, ladies and gents, and do what works for you.

Peace!

Keep the Game Going Online

Head Over to the *Cutting Corners* Website

If you're looking for more material, head over to:

http://www.cuttingcornersbook.com

We'll keep the site updated regularly, and keep you informed with the latest news on the book.

The *Cutting Corners* Review Sheet

Since we've covered so much ground, I've also assembled a single-page PDF review sheet for the book that you can get online. If you need to reference a quick overview of the main points we've gone through, this is your ticket.

Get it here for free:

http://www.cuttingcornersbook.com/reviewsheet

You can print the sheet out, or you can download it to your smartphone (instructions for how to do that are on the website.)

You can also e-mail me directly at **justin@cuttingcornersbook.com** if you want to send me any feedback. I'd love to hear everything you have to say.

www.ingramcontent.com/pod-product-compliance
Lightning Source LLC
Chambersburg PA
CBHW071501040426
42444CB00008B/1447